KOREA THE BEAUTIFUL:
TREASURES OF THE HERMIT KINGDOM

This book is available at a special discount
when ordered in bulk quantities. For more
information contact: Dr. Yushin Yoo, 1005 Westgate Dr., Murray, Ky. 42071
Tel: (502) 753-6291 or 762-4420

U.S. Library of Congress Cataloging in Publication Data

YOO, YUSHIN
Korea the Beautiful: Treasures of the Hermit Kingdom

Includes appendices and indexes
SUMMARY: An introduction to the cultural history of Korea,
traditions, description and travel, and way of life of the people of Korea.

1. Korea-Civilization 2. Korea-History. 3. Korea-
Social life and customs. 4. Korea-Description and travel.
I. Title.

DS 902.4. Y64 1987   915.19   LC 86-083328
ISBN 0-942091-01-9

Printed in the Republic of Korea
Samsung Moonhwa Printing Co.
36-45, 4ga, Ch'ungmu-ro, Chung-ku,
Seoul, Korea TLX: STPRINT K27793 FAX: (02) 273-6042
Tel: (02) 267-6191/3 or 266-0698

Published by

Dae Won Press
152-3, Myo-Dong, Chongno-Ku,
Seoul, Korea.
Tel: (02) 742-1677, 762-6998

This book is dedicated to my parents,
Rev. Eul Sul Yoo and Shoon Hi Choi.

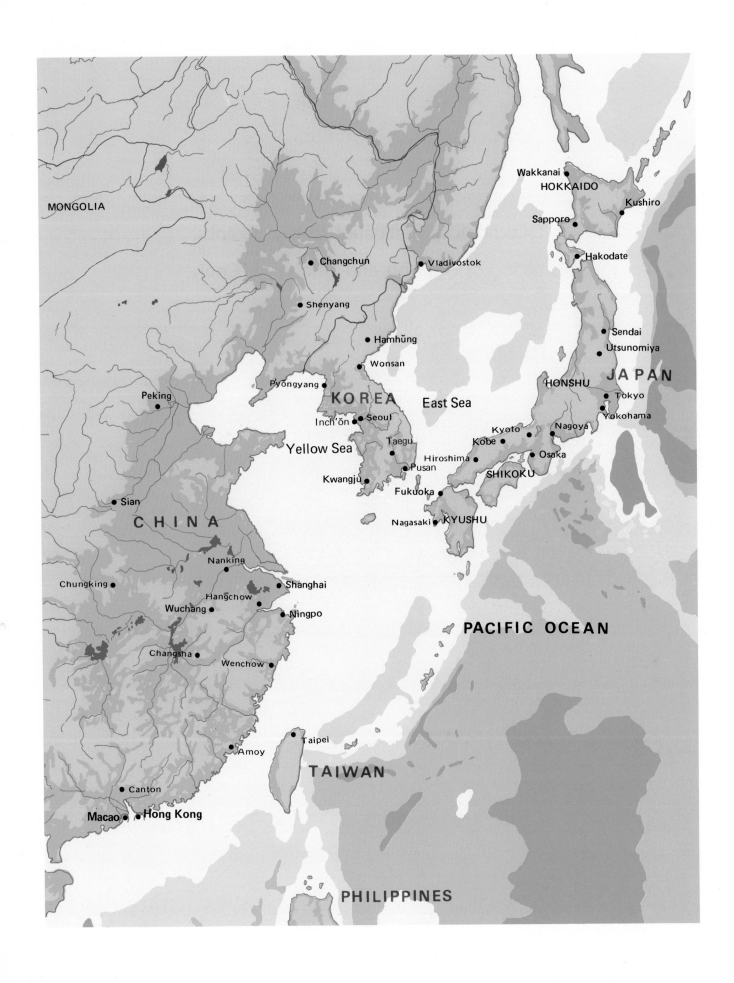

PREFACE

With the 1988 World Olympic Games scheduled to be held in Seoul, Korea, more attention will be focused on Korea, its land, its people, and its culture by the news media and the public at large. For the public seeking more detailed information, this book should be timely. Also many Korean immigrants in the United States have expressed a desire for such a publication to show to their children and friends.

My work is intended to be an introduction for the general reader to the uniqueness of Korean culture, emphasizing some of the best national treasures, with special highlights on ten of the most scenic national parks.

I would like to express my gratitude to the Committee on Institutional Studies and Research at Murray State University, who granted me the research funds to complete my work for this book during the summer of 1986. I wish also to express my appreciation to Mr. Taewan Yu, Assistant Minister for Overseas Information Service, and his other staff members, Mr. Moon Gyo Chung, Director of the Production Division, and his assistant Mr. Sungsam Sin. Their office provided much valuable assistance in my endeavor.

I am especially grateful to several outstanding professors at Murray State University and want to give particular thanks to Dr. Michael M. Cohen, Professor of English and to Dr. Kenneth Wolf, Professor of History, who both reviewed this work and gave me so many valuable suggestions and critical comments to improve it.

Special thanks to Ms. Teresa Ragsdale who assisted me with various tasks in preparing the manuscript.

The working scholar is too often a distracted husband and father. During the summer while I was writing the text of this book, my five-year-old son, Chris, repeatedly interrupted my thoughts with numerous questions and requests for attention. One day after several attempts at being patient, I gave vent to my frustrations and told Chris very sternly that I was very busy with important work and that he was to leave me alone. He withdrew and peace and quiet had priority at last. Before many minutes had passed, however, Chris returned to my study carrying his Lego toys. He set them down nearby and turned to tell me very solemnly, "Daddy, I am going to be very busy building with my Lego. Please leave me alone."

Murray, Kentucky
November 1986

Yushin Yoo

CONTENTS

Chronological Table

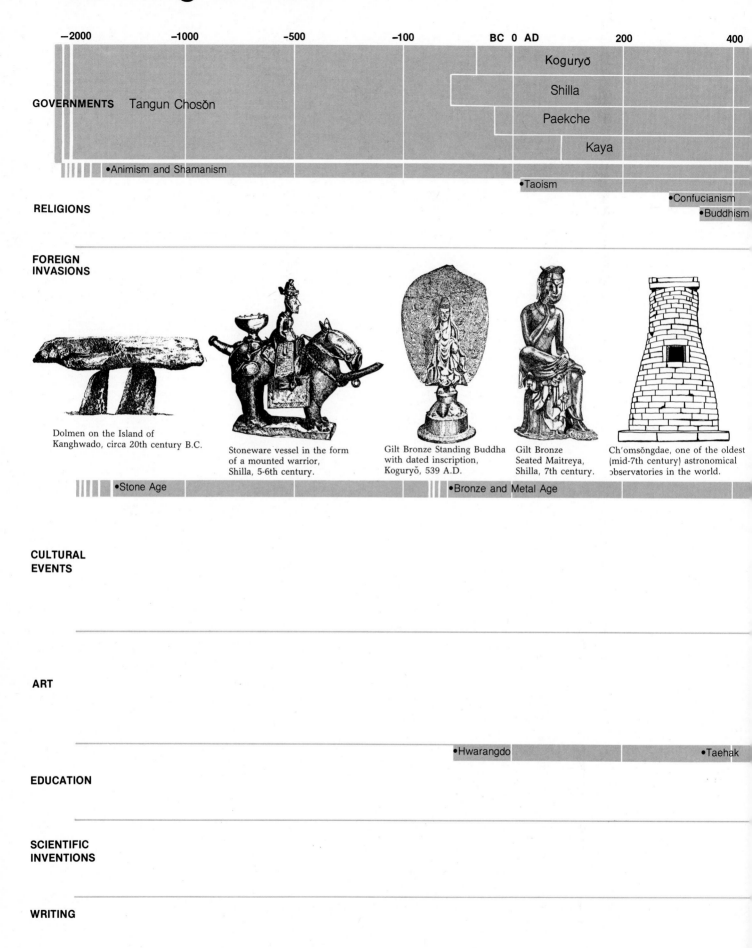

	−2000	−1000	−500	−100	BC 0 AD	200	400
GOVERNMENTS	Tangun Chosŏn				Koguryŏ		
					Shilla		
					Paekche		
					Kaya		

•Animism and Shamanism

•Taoism

•Confucianism

•Buddhism

RELIGIONS

FOREIGN INVASIONS

Dolmen on the Island of Kanghwado, circa 20th century B.C.

Stoneware vessel in the form of a mounted warrior, Shilla, 5-6th century.

Gilt Bronze Standing Buddha with dated inscription, Koguryŏ, 539 A.D.

Gilt Bronze Seated Maitreya, Shilla, 7th century.

Ch'omsŏngdae, one of the oldest (mid-7th century) astronomical observatories in the world.

•Stone Age

•Bronze and Metal Age

CULTURAL EVENTS

ART

•Hwarangdo

•Taehak

EDUCATION

SCIENTIFIC INVENTIONS

WRITING

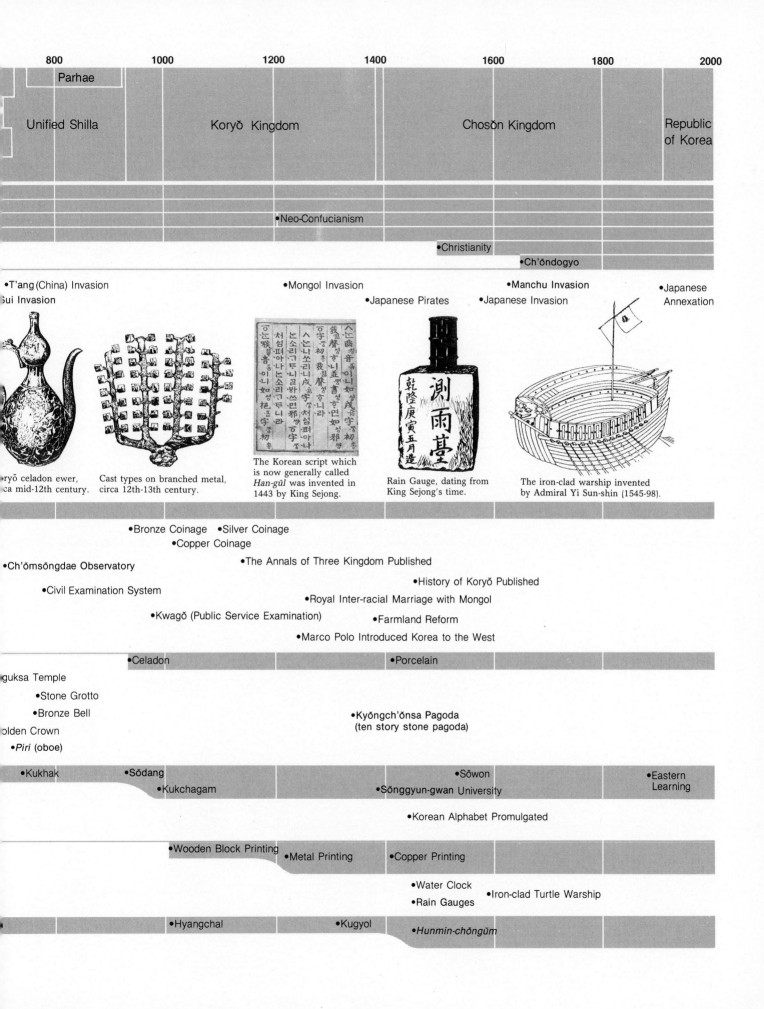

| 800 | 1000 | 1200 | 1400 | 1600 | 1800 | 2000 |

Parhae

Unified Shilla | Koryŏ Kingdom | Chosŏn Kingdom | Republic of Korea

•Neo-Confucianism

•Christianity

•Ch'ŏndogyo

•T'ang (China) Invasion   •Mongol Invasion   •Manchu Invasion   •Japanese Annexation

Sui Invasion   •Japanese Pirates   •Japanese Invasion

Koryŏ celadon ewer, ca mid-12th century.

Cast types on branched metal, circa 12th-13th century.

The Korean script which is now generally called *Han-gŭl* was invented in 1443 by King Sejong.

Rain Gauge, dating from King Sejong's time.

The iron-clad warship invented by Admiral Yi Sun-shin (1545-98).

•Bronze Coinage   •Silver Coinage

•Copper Coinage

•Ch'ŏmsŏngdae Observatory   •The Annals of Three Kingdom Published

•History of Koryŏ Published

•Civil Examination System

•Royal Inter-racial Marriage with Mongol

•Kwagŏ (Public Service Examination)   •Farmland Reform

•Marco Polo Introduced Korea to the West

•Celadon   •Porcelain

guksa Temple

•Stone Grotto   •Kyŏngch'ŏnsa Pagoda (ten story stone pagoda)

•Bronze Bell

olden Crown

•*Piri* (oboe)

•Kukhak   •Sŏdang   •Sŏwon   •Eastern Learning

•Kukchagam   •Sŏnggyun-gwan University

•Korean Alphabet Promulgated

•Wooden Block Printing   •Metal Printing   •Copper Printing

•Water Clock

•Iron-clad Turtle Warship

•Rain Gauges

•Hyangchal   •Kugyol   •*Hunmin-chŏngŭm*

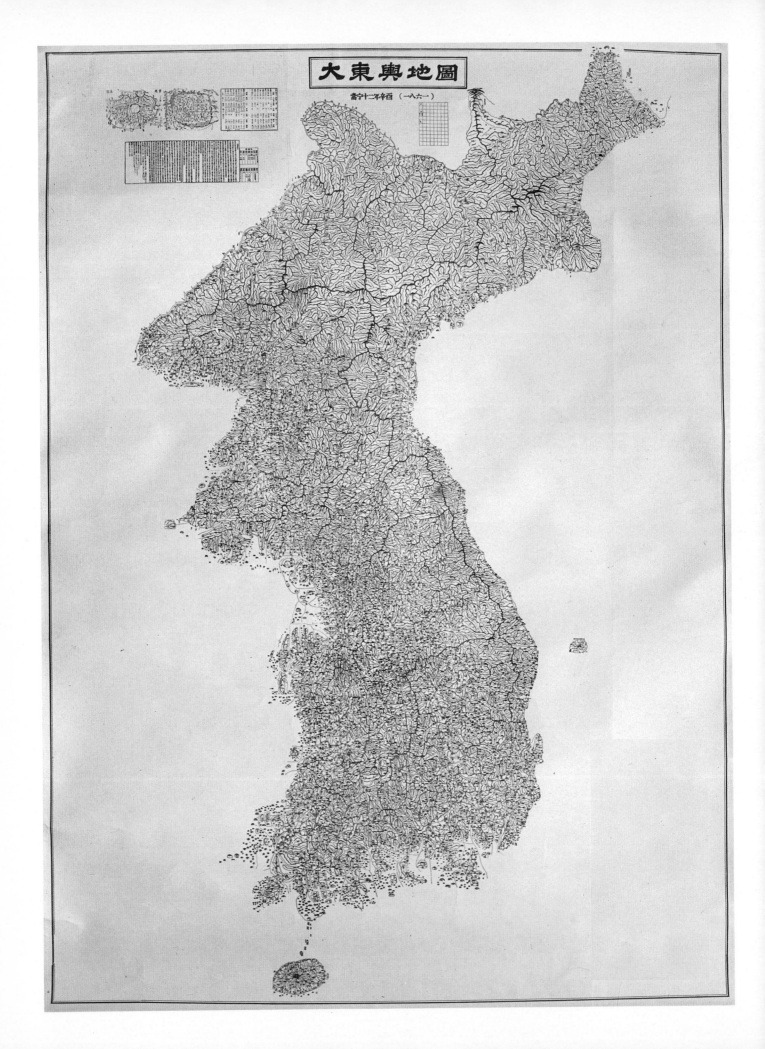

INTRODUCTION

The Korean people, as far back as history records and probably much further, have inhabited a peninsula extending due south of Manchuria, curving gently east and then west, forming a rabbit-like shape. They possess a culturally unique, homogeneous national identity, closely related to, yet independent of that of their powerful neighbors, China and Japan. A small country with a distinctive history and culture, influenced in part by others, but having its unique stamp, Korea has maintained its national identity. Throughout history Koreans have been victims of foreign attacks but the spirit of the Korean race and nation has never ceased.

The legendary past of the nation stretches back nearly 5,000 years. According to historical records the Korean people's sphere of activities once covered Shantung and Shansi provinces in China and almost the entire territory of Manchuria.

By the time of the Three Kingdoms (57 B.C.–668 A.D.) their domain extended from the Chekang Province in China to the Japanese Islands, the northern portion occupied by the Koguryŏ Kingdom and the southern part occupied by the Shilla and the Paekche kingdoms, in the east and in the west, respectively.

The three-way struggle among the three kingdoms for supremacy over the entire Korean peninsula raged for nearly 700 years until 668 when the Shilla Kingdom conquered the Koguryŏ Kingdom, having conquered the Paekche Kingdom five years before. At that time the Korean peninsula was unified with approximately the same borders as those of the present day.

The Shilla kings presided over a cultural renaissance as brilliant as it was relatively brief. At this time, the Korean kings established a "younger brother" relationship with the emperors of China unlike any form of international linkage earlier known in the Orient. Korean culture came to incorporate the cultures not only of China and of various tribes of northeast Asia, but also of many other tribes living west of the Chinese mainland. The archeological remnants left behind by this ancient kingdom include remarkable jewelry, pottery and Buddhist relics still to be seen around the ancient capital city, Kyŏngju.

Buddhist influence entered Korean culture mostly through China. Thus the philosophy of Buddhism presented itself as an entirely new world of thought to the Korean people, mostly through Chinese characters. These borrowings were modified to suit local conditions, and eventually were passed on to Japan. By the end of the Shilla period, Buddhist culture had become indelibly stamped on Korea, so much so that it came to be identified almost wholly with Korean culture.

The long years of peace and prosperity after the unification of the Korean peninsula by the Shilla Kingdom, however, led to the decadence of the nobility and to the rise of powerful clan chieftains who weakened the power of the Shilla kings.

General Wang Kŏn was one of those military chieftains who helped to defeat the Shilla Kingdom and who succeeded in founding a new

This map, Taedong Yŏjido, was made by Kim Chŏng-ho in 1861 during the reign of King Ch'ŏlchong. Kim and his daughter spent about 30 years traveling around the country on foot to collect information to make the map, which is on a piece of wood. Today's topographers are amazed at the accuracy of the map which was made using only a compass and cloth tape measures.

11

kingdom named Koryŏ, from which the present English appellation of ''Korea'' is derived. The last king of Shilla offered his kingdom to General Wang Kŏn, signifying the peaceful transfer of government.

The Koryŏ Kingdom ruled the peninsula for 475 years, through a succession of 34 kings. Buddhism flourished as the state religion, and social and ethical principles of Confucian origin served as the moral standards. Innumerable temples were built throughout the country, and the arts found ready expression in Buddhist sculpture, painting, architecture and literature. The people of Koryŏ succeeded in developing a Buddhist world of their own, as evidenced by publication of the mammoth *Tripitaka Koreana*, historically significant as the first example of woodcut, block-type printing.

The publication of the *Tripitaka Koreana* was begun in 1011 by royal command of the eighth Koryŏ king, Hyŏnjong, from more than 5,000 volumes of Buddhist scripture imported from China. It took more than 16 years to engrave all the woodblocks necessary to complete the project, which eventually comprised more than 6,000 volumes. Later, in 1232, movable, metal printing type was invented and used for the first time in the world in Koryŏ, over 200 years before Gutenberg first used movable lead-cast printing type in Germany in 1450.

The Koryŏ civilization flourished for many centuries during which the first civil service examination system was inaugurated, schools for education of the young were established, and taxation laws were instituted to stabilize national revenues.

During this era bronze coins were used, and the art of printing was

One of the more than 80,000 woodblocks carved during the 13th century for printing the **Tripitaka Koreana.**

highly developed. Koryŏ was renowned for its highly refined celadon ceramics, considered by many the most graceful ever made by man and still treasured in museums around the world.

Continual harassment of Koryŏ by northern invaders of central Asia, who had conquered China and who threatened both central Europe and Japan, was climaxed by the Mongol invasion of the kingdom in the 13th century when the Mongols crossed the Yalu River and marched on the capital city of Kaesŏng, the present day P'yŏngyang. Pressed hard, Koryŏ finally concluded a peace treaty under which the Koryŏ king accepted the overlordship of the Mongol Khan. The Mongols eventually withdrew after the failure of their invasion armada to subdue Japan, but their continuing influence at the Korean court resulted in political splits and eventually in a revolt in support of renewed nationalism. The Chosŏn Kingdom was established in 1392.

General Yi Sŏng-gye, enthroned as the first king of the new kingdom in 1392, moved the capital city from Kaesŏng to the site of the present day Seoul. The early period of the kingdom brought major reforms in political and social structures. Buddhism, which had once wielded great power during the previous kingdom, gave way to Confucianism, which the new kingdom espoused as the state cult.

Remarkable cultural strides were made during the first 70 years of the Chosŏn Kingdom. The man most responsible for the brilliant age of culture was King Sejong, the most enlightened ruler of the kingdom. His encouragement and personal interest led to many scientific and technological inventions and cultural innovations.

King Sejong first developed the Korean language and "han-gŭl," the Korean alphabet of 28 letters, which was later reduced to the present 24 letters. It was simple in form and of such phonetic adaptability and clarity that anyone could learn to read and write it in a very short time. He also made contributions to the study of astronomy by constructing sundials and astronomical observatories. With the aid of scholars many literary works were published in the native language he had fostered.

In the 16th century, the Chosŏn Kingdom suffered its first foreign invasion by Japan. Toyotomi Hideyoshi, the new shogun of Japan at that time, requested the Chosŏn government to grant his troops free passage up the Korean peninsula to facilitate their planned invasion of Manchuria and China. The Japanese answered the Korean refusal with an invasion in 1592. The Japanese took less than three weeks to capture Seoul after disembarking at Pusan.

With Korea's very existence thus at stake, there emerged a great national hero, Admiral Yi Sun-shin, who invented the "turtle warship" (Kŏbuksŏn), the first ironclad warship in the world's history. With a fleet of these turtle warships he attacked the huge flotilla of Japanese vessels and defeated the enemy in battle after battle. The Japanese were finally driven back to their own shores.

During the next 300 years the Chosŏn Kingdom shut itself off completely from the rest of the world, largely because the invasion by the Japanese and the subsequent aggression by the Manchus showed how troublesome it was to live in open contact with warlike neighbors. This was a period of the "Korean dark ages," a period during which Korea came to be known as the Hermit Kingdom.

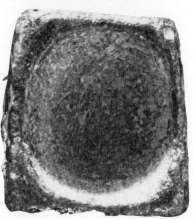

Bronze type head (top) and tail (bottom), 12th-13th century. The earliest movable metal type was invented in Korea during the 12th century.

13

A replica of the world's first ironclad warship, the Kŏbuksŏn, or "Turtle Ship," invented by Admiral Yi Sunshin in the 16th century.

Despite remarkable achievements such as the invention of movable printing type, an efficient phonetic Korean alphabet to replace the Chinese ideographs, and the success of the ironclad warships, by the late 19th century Korea found herself in no position to resist, or even properly comprehend, the encroachments of Western technology, trade, and imperialism.

The Chosŏn Kingdom basked in complacent isolationism until 1866 when Western influence was physically felt. First there occurred the state persecution of Catholics, including the execution of nine French Jesuits. The French government dispatched a punitive fleet to Korea which was driven back by Korean soldiers. Then in 1871, an American flotilla under Admiral Rodgers was sent to repeat Commodore Perry's exploits in Japan. But it was Japan, the latecomer on the scene, which succeeded in opening Korea in 1876. This was soon followed in 1882 by a treaty with the United States and other major powers contending in the area. Korea thus became the scene of bitter rivalry for domination among Russians, Japanese, and Chinese because of the strategic importance of the peninsula's location, as well as its potential for exploitation. Japan emerged victorious over the others by defeating China in 1890 and then Russia in 1904.

Japan annexed Korea on August 29, 1910, in the 4243rd year after the legendary founding of Korea by Tan-gun, thus putting an end to the 500-year-old Chosŏn Kingdom. Then began a 36-year "dark age," during which the Japanese made every effort to erase any trace of Korean national identity, even to the extent of forbidding use of the national language, burning all the books written in Korean, and attempting to substitute Japanese names for all personal Korean names. Koreans, however, were not entirely without hope for the restoration of their independence. In March 1919 Koreans raised a nationwide peaceful protest demonstration against Japanese rule, hoping for support from the Versailles Peace Conference, which had trumpeted national self-determination as a principle of international law. This provoked further brutal persecution by the Japanese, but attracted virtually no notice abroad. However, the occasion served symbolically to focus the Koreans' new sense of nationalism and independence. The independence movement was advanced from time to time by students or religious groups protesting Japanese rule, until it ended in 1945 with the defeat of Japan at the end of World War II.

No sooner had the Korean people heard the bells of liberation ring in 1945 than they found their fatherland divided into two parts at the 38th parallel. The northern half of the peninsula fell into the hands of Russia, and Americans held the south. Provisions contained in the Cairo Declaration and later resolutions of the United Nations in September 1947 insured general elections in Korea under United Nations supervision. In accordance with the resolutions, the United Nations Commission for Korea was dispatched to Seoul in January 1948 to supervise the elections under which a unified Korean government would be formed. However, North Korea, which had rejected the United Nations resolutions, obstructed the entry of the United Nations Commission into North Korea, and the general elections were held only in the area south of the 38th parallel to which the commission had access.

On August 15, 1948, three years after Korea was liberated, the government of the Republic of Korea (ROK) was officially proclaimed. The United Nations approved the Republic of Korea as the legitimate government in the South.

The Korean War, a most tragic period of fratricide for the Korean nation, broke out on June 25, 1950, less than two years after the establishment of the governments. To North Korea's suprise 16 nations, acting under a United Nations resolution, assisted South Korea in the fight against aggression. However, Red China entered the fighting on the side of the North, and the war reached a stalemate, ending with a negotiated truce signed in 1953, setting up a demilitarized zone (DMZ) close to the 38th parallel, consisting of a 249.5-kilometer long Military Demarcation Line cutting across the waist of the Korean peninsula.

In the Republic of Korea, recovery from wartime devastation was slow until the 1960 expulsion of the aged and authoritarian president, Syngman Rhee. After a year of political confusion during which many unruly demonstrations occurred and two governments attempted to restore order, an army junta siezed power in a peaceful coup, instituted rigorous, long overdue reforms, and eventually restored democratic civilian government in 1963.

During the past decade, progress in all fields has been rapid. Though still menaced by a belligerent North Korean neighbor, South Koreans now face the world with fresh confidence, pride, and optimism, based on the factors that have kept them one nation and one people for so long: a common language and culture, a clear sense of national identity, and a stubborn determination to shape their own destiny.

Part One
Geographical Overview

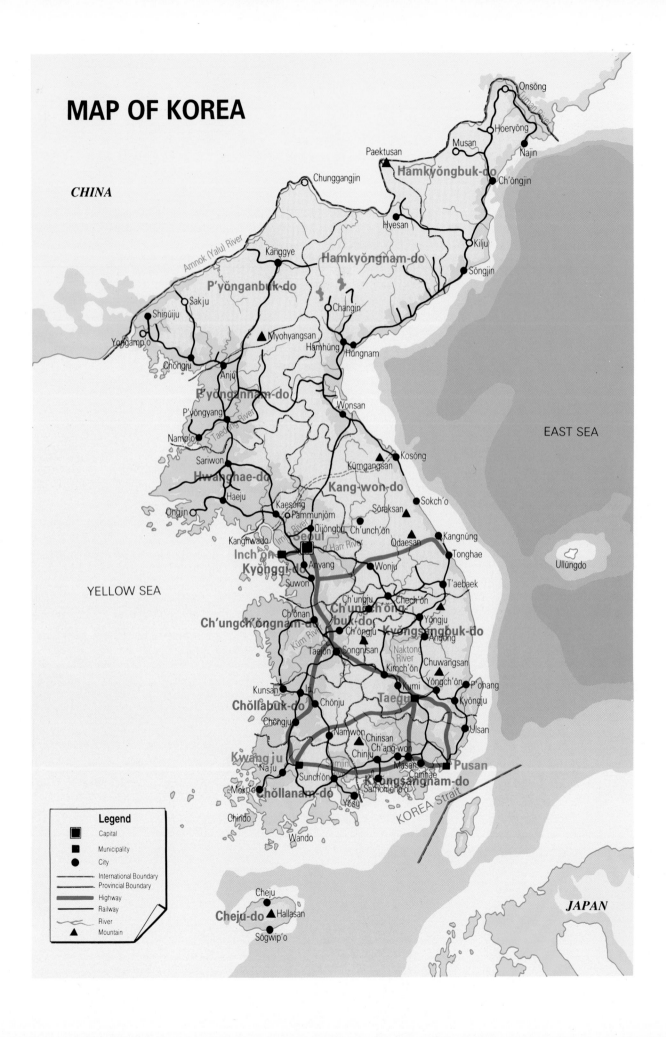

The Land

The Korean peninsula, stretching almost directly south from Manchuria, is approximately 966 kilometers long from north to south and includes some 3,300 islands scattered along the 8,694-kilometer-long coast. About 200 islands are habitable. The land is bounded by Manchuria and Siberia on the north, by the East China Sea on the east, by the narrow Korea Strait on the south, and by the Yellow Sea on the west. It is about 114 kilometers wide at its narrowest point and has an average width from east to west of about 386 kilometers. It is separated from China's Shantung peninsula to the west by a 188-kilometer-wide expanse of the Yellow Sea and from Manchuria on the northwest by the Yalu or Amnok-gang River, and from Russia on the northeast by the Tumen or Tuman-gang River. The shortest distance between Korea and Japan is 204 kilometers.

The peninsula and all of its associated islands lie between 124°11' and 131°55' east longitude and between 33°7' and 43°1' south latitude. The standard time is based on the meridian passing through the center of the peninsula along 127°3' east longitude. The time difference with Washington, D.C. is ten hours, and with London, eight hours.

The peninsular area is about 223,600 square kilometers. The land is presently divided into two parts along the 38th parallel, the Republic of Korea in the south and the Democratic People's Republic of Korea in the north. The Republic of Korea's administrative control covers about 45 percent of the total peninsular area.

A very large part of the agricultural land of Korea lies on its south side and all the long and navigable rivers are in the south. The majority of the harbors are on the Yellow Sea. Geographically Korea seems to face toward Manchuria and China to the west and Russian Siberia to the north with her back toward Japan.

Due to its geographical location, forming a bridge connecting the islands to the south and the land mass to the north, Korea has been an international thoroughfare. In fact, Korea in ancient times was a sort of relay station, transmitting to Japan the brilliant culture of China.

The major portion of the country is characterized by hills and mountains which account for nearly 80 percent of its territory. Many of these mountains are the result of volcanoes, for example the highest of them, Mt. Paektusan, or "Mount of Eternal Snow," in the extinct crater of which now lies a lake. Volcanic action also created many hot springs throughout the country. Most parts of the peninsula were formed on a granite foundation, and most mountains are made of beautiful sandstone, marble and other building stones.

Low hills are predominant in the south and west and gradually yield to higher mountains in the east and north. Thus the western and southern slopes are gradual and meet with plains, low hills and winding river basins, while the eastern slopes plunge directly into the nearby East Sea.

The Nangnim Sanmaek Mountain Range in the north and their southern extension, the T'aebaek Sanmaek Mountain Range, form the east-west peninsula division and the watershed along the east coast. While rarely exceeding a height of 1,200 meters, the numerous peaks form a rugged, steep terrain. The "roof of Korea," the Kaema Plateau, has an average elevation of 1,500 meters above sea level. Mt. Paektusan, located in the northwestern corner of the plateau is the highest peak at 2,744 meters.

19

Autumn colors are sometimes muted
by the mists that form around the peaks
of Mt. Sŏraksan at sundown.

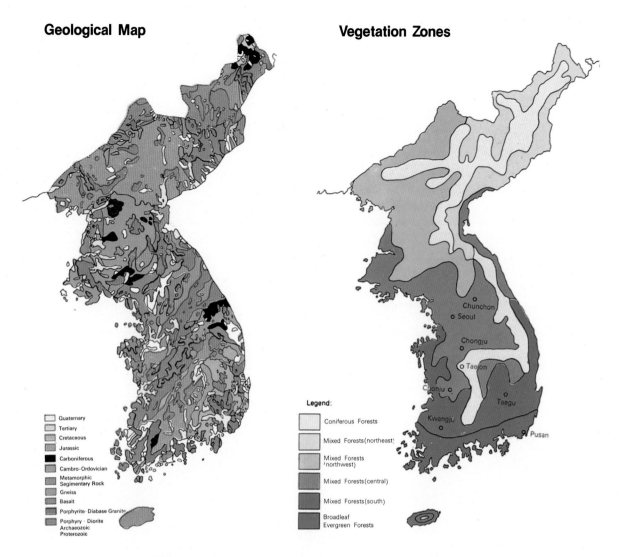

Geological Map

Legend:
- Quaternary
- Tertiary
- Cretaceous
- Jurassic
- Carboniferous
- Cambro-Ordovician
- Metamorphic Segimentary Rock
- Gneiss
- Basalt
- Porphyrite · Diabase Granite
- Porphyry · Diorite Archaeozoic Proterozoic

Vegetation Zones

Legend:
- Coniferous Forests
- Mixed Forests (northeast)
- Mixed Forests (northwest)
- Mixed Forests (central)
- Mixed Forests (south)
- Broadleaf Evergreen Forests

Chunchon
Seoul
Chongju
Taejon
Chonju
Taegu
Kwangju
Pusan

Many of Korea's highest summits occur along the Nangnim Sanmaek and T'aebaek Sanmaek ranges: Mt. Nangnimsan (2,014m), Mt. Kŭmgangsan (1,638m), Mt. Sŏraksan (1,708m) and Mt. T'aebaeksan (1,546m). These peaks form a spectacular panorama of granite pinnacles and deep narrow canyons with many waterfalls and rapids. Lesser ranges and lateral spurs insure that one is seldom out of sight of mountains anywhere on the peninsula.

The peninsula as a whole is "tilted," lifted in the east and somewhat sunken in the west and south, a process that began in the late Mesozoic Era. Thus the east coast is a nearly unbroken, precipitous shoreline of cliffs and rocks where the T'aebaek Sanmaek rear up from the sea. Beaches are usually found where streams empty into the sea, often taking the form of coastal lagoons enclosed by sand spits and bars. The emergent shoreline and relatively short tidal range make these beaches and their facing waters particularly clean and popular. Ullŭngdo is the largest of the few islands off the east coast. The west and south coasts are extremely irregular shorelines as the rolling terrain follows the peninsular tilt into the East Sea and Pacific waters. Most of Korea's 3,400 islands are the result of these nearly hidden ridges and mountains, the most notable exception being the inactive volcanic island of Chejudo, some 138 kilometers off the southwest coast.

The Pacific tidal currents force themselves into the Yellow Sea, thus forming a tidal range of 6 to 10 meters and broad mud flats along the west and southwest coasts, as well as such fine harbors as Inch'ŏn.

A rocky cliff on Chejudo Island.

Most of the peninsula's myriad islands are found off the southern and southwestern shores. The length of the southern coastline is nearly eight times its straight-line measurement. The mud flats common to the west coast are also found on the western third of the southern coast, while the eastern and central portions show submerged, almost fiord-like valleys and a much lessened tidal range, which results in the fine harbors of Pusan and Mokp'o, as well as broad, clean beaches.

Most of Korea's rivers flow into the Yellow Sea and the Pacific waters to the south after draining the gentler western and southern slopes of the peninsula. The streams that do flow east from the T'aebaek Divide are short, straight and fast.

The gradual descent to the west and south has resulted in a relatively large number of streams for a territory the size of Korea. Five rivers exceed 400 kilometers in channel length: the Amnokkang River (790km), the Tuman-gang River (521km), the Han-gang River (514km), the Kŭmgang River (401km) and the Naktonggang River (521km). In summer the rivers swell with the rainfall which accompanies the monsoon, often flooding valley plains once or twice a year. In other seasons the plains are relatively dry.

In modern times the rivers have become increasingly important as sources of irrigation water. More than 70 percent of Korea's rice fields depend on river water irrigation, and large-scale, multipurpose dams provide flood control and produce electricity, as well as industrial water supplies.

23

Tokto, an island off the east coast, is famous for fantastic rock formations.

Climate

Although Korea has a traditional climate halfway between the continental and the marine, the climate is nearer to the continental type than that of the marine countries located in corresponding latitudes. The climate of Korea may be compared with that of northeastern America between the same latitudes, the only difference being that in Korea the month of July brings the rainy season.

The average annual temperature in Korea seems slightly lower than in some other countries of corresponding latitudes, but the difference is felt only in winter in northern Korea. In general the temperature is somewhat similar to that of the eastern part of the United States between Maine and South Carolina.

The average temperature throughout the year is 13°C (55°F) along the southern coast, while it drops as low as 10°C and 8°C (50°F and 46°F) respectively over the mid and northern climatic zones.

Differences in temperature are least conspicious during summer. The average temperature in August in the lower area of the east coast, which is affected by the warm currents of the East Sea, is about 25°C (77°F),

Climatic Calendar

MAR.	APR.	MAY	JUNE	JULY	AUG.	SEP.	OCT.	NOV.	DEC.	JAN.	FEB.
SPRING			SUMMER				AUTUMN		WINTER		
North-west Monsoon	Transition period		South-west Monsoon[7]				Transition period	North-West Monsoon			
Yellow wind[2]			Rainy season		Bonin High predominates	24 hour precip exceeds 30.5 cm owing to typhoon	Under influence of migratory high, elongated east-west mean track along 38° N.[10]		Heavy snow may be expected along Taebaeksan Mts. with strong north to south pressure gradient (high to north)		
Foehn[1]		Late frost[3]	Polar front south of ROK	Heavy Rain[8]							
Blocking due to slow-moving Mongolian high results in cut-off low over Yellow Sea.			Pressure higher to east.	High pressure area to south; low to north.				High pressure area to west; low to east.			
Korea under influence of migratory high[4]				Typhoons may affect ROK.[9]			Exceptionally good visibility over long distance within migratory high area.[11]		'3 cold and 4 warm day cycle' prevails over Korea.		
Gust winds[5]	Frontal thunderstorms duration 1-2 hrs. up to twice per month.[6]		Airmass thunderstorms, 5-10 km. diameter; 2-5 per month.			Frontal thunderstorms, 0-2/month	Shanghai low may develop and affect ROK.		Taiwan lows frequently affect ROK.		
Taiwan lows											
Sea fog, most frequent in July over Inch'ŏn area. Frontal and radiation fog may occur occasionally.				Radiation and frontal fogs occur frequently, however duration is short. Radiation fog seen inland.					Siberian airmass dominates Korea.		

[1] North China low passing over North Korea causes foehn (hot, dry south to easterly flow) over west and central sectors of ROK.
[2] Mongolian low passing over southern Manchuria causes yellow winds (strong, dry west wind carrying yellow dust).
[3] Late frost may occur when migratory high predominates over ROK.
[4] Mean track of migratory high is along 33°N
[5] Low over Shantung Peninsula may cause gusty winds over ROK.
[6] Intense frontal thunderstorms in May signal approach of rainy season.
[7] Cool summer and drought if South-west Monsoon weak and Okhotsk High intense.
[8] Heavy rain latter part of rainy season.
[9] Hot and humid with maritime tropical air intrusion. None or as many as two tropical storms or typhoons from end of June through September may affect ROK; least likely in August owing to Bonin High.
[10] Migratory highs move at about 20 knots, speed up with northward movement and vice versa.
[11] Often precedes bad weather.

while it falls to about 21°C (70°F) in the northern part of the northeastern coast and the Kaema Plateau.

The hottest period of the year lasts about one month, starting early in August. The temperature then is close to that of the tropical zone, and it is much hotter in the midland and the areas below than in the rest of the country. The area around Taegu is the hottest region in Korea, with the temperature going up as high as 40°C (104°F).

Despite its small size the Korean peninsula shows a wide range of climate. While parts of the south are subtropical, the far north has a climate much like that of Siberia. In the summer moist air drifts in from over the sea; in the winter dry, cold air drifts outward from the continent of Asia.

Around Seoul, the capital of the Republic of Korea, which lies about halfway down the western side of the peninsula, the climate is moderate. The hottest summer months have an average temperature of 25°C (77°F) and the coldest winter months −5°C (23°F).

In winter, the mountains and hills are snow-clad and the rivers frozen. The winter lasts for six months in the northern part, but for only three months in the southern provinces.

Rainfall

The average annual rainfall is about 800-1,500 millimeters. Almost half of the rainfall comes during the summer months, June, July, and August. The rainfall of Korea is about twice that of the mainland of China and half the amount usually registered in Japan. During the winter months, which are from October through March, there is very little precipitation and this is called the dry season. Then in the months of April and May the precipitation increases and in June through August it rains almost half of the total annual precipitation. This means that Korea has about 305-508 millimeters of rainfall during the summer months.

Climate and Rainfall : Climate (C) Rainfall (mm)

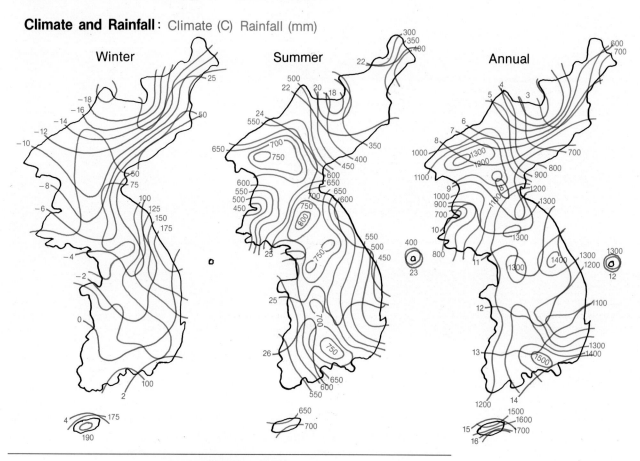

CLIMATE OF KOREA

Cities	Average Temp. (°C)			H&L		Preciptiation (mm)				
	Jan.	July	Annual	High	Low	Annual	July	August	July & August	Wet Days
Sŏngjin	−5.8	22.1	8.1	37.5	−24.6	703	103	163	37.8	105
Chunggangjin	−2.1	21.6	3.7	38.6	−43.1	818	176	183	31.7	131
Shinŭiju	−9.8	24.1	8.7	36.9	−27.7	818	176	183	31.7	100
Wonsan	−3.8	23.8	10.3	39.6	−21.9	1328	270	320	44.6	117
P'yŏngyang	−8.2	24.4	9.3	37.2	−28.2	941	243	232	50.5	108
Seoul	−4.9	25.5	11.0	38.2	−23.1	1246	366	250	49.5	112
Inch'ŏn	−3.9	25.0	10.8	38.9	−21.0	1043	286 .	206	45.9	105
Taegu	−1.7	26.0	12.5	40.0	−20.2	970	299	157	37.7	90
Chŏnju	−2.0	26.0	12.2	38.2	−17.8	1233	299	249	44.4	125
Kwangju	−1.1	25.4	13.9	37.6	−19.4	1243	261	219	38.6	128
Pusan	−1.9	25.6	13.6	36.0	−14.0	1399	279	179	32.7	101
Mokp'o	0.9	26.1	13.2	37.0	−14.0	1065	197	166	34.1	128
Cheju	4.6	25.9	13.3	87.5	−50.7	1382	206	216	30.7	141

Crystal clear streams, fantastic rocks and cliffs and beautiful waterfalls characterize the principal resort area in Mt. Sŏraksan.

The Four Seasons and Their Traditional Festivities

Korea has four very distinctive or clearly identifiable seasons: spring (March-May), summer (June-August), autumn (September-October), and winter (December-February).

SPRING: MARCH-MAY

Spring comes with the pink of flowering azaleas and cherry blossoms on the hillside and is specially heralded when the swallows, migratory birds from the south, arrive to start building their nests. By April most of the atmospheric activity moves from over the continent out to the ocean. The cold winds from the high pressure areas over Siberia are no longer dominant. The ocean's warmer winds and high pressure turn the sky clear and bring warmer temperatures. Whenever the high pressure air meets a cold front, one of the very frequent spring rains is produced. Some southern cities such as Pusan and Cheju have as much as 406 millimeters of rainfall in the spring. Rainfall increases gradually for three months. Though slight, it is adequate for preparing seedbeds for rice, for sowing spring vegetables, and for planting summer crops such as barley, corn and soybeans. The average temperature at this time of the year is about 10°-16°C (50°-60°F).

Winds are characterized by varied directions and in early spring are more gusty and dusty from the northwest, but as late spring approaches the moist airstreams start blowing from the south. May is one of Korea's sunniest and most pleasant months.

One of the most famous festivities of the springtime is called Tano Day, the fifth day of the fifth lunar month. According to ancient customs, on this day people rest from their work, dress up in their best and feast as they do on New Year's Day.

At home, a feast is prepared, and the family visits the ancestors' burial ground to observe a memorial service. The origin of this holiday is presumed to be the rites observed by ancient Koreans after the spring seed-planting to the "heavenly gods" for a good harvest in the fall.

People, especially women, like to wash their hair with calamus water on this day. The most spectacular scene celebrating the Tano holiday is that of maidens swinging high and low against the sky in a contest. In the swing contest whoever can swing the highest and kick a suspended bell wins prizes of chests, bureaus, mirrors and other household goods. While the womenfolk are exhibiting their skills at swinging, the men demonstrate their physical powers in wrestling matches, in which a bull is traditionally first prize, a hog, second, and a chicken, third.

Chejudo Island becomes a golden paradise when rape flowers bloom in spring.

SUMMER: JUNE-AUGUST

Summers in Korea are hot and rainy. By late June or early July the monsoon develops. The entire country is dominated by the warm, moist sea wind from directions almost opposite those of the winter winds. As this warm air moves over mountains onto shore, it brings rain. By July this onshore flow of air is well established and persists until the latter part of September. When the monsoon season starts usually there are no more than three clear days the whole month of July. This calm rain and high temperature normally lasts for about five weeks. During this rainy season, rivers and streams throughout Korea are filled with run-off water from the upper streams, which often causes floods. By late July the hot weather temperature may reach about 31°-38°C (90°-100°F), but the average temperature for the country as a whole at this time of the year holds around 21°-27°C (70°-80°F). Abundant rainfall and the hot summer are necessary for growing rice. Inadequate rainfall or the late arrival of the rainy season is liable to cause failure of the rice crops.

The rainfall and humidity will decrease by late August. By late summer the rice paddies begin to ripen and yellow, the heat starts to settle down, the rains are over, and harvest time is approaching. The only dark spots in the sky are the clouds that mark the approach of typhoons from the Pacific. They come most often in September, but usually they miss Korea.

Falling during the summer, usually in July and/or August, are three days called Ch'obok, Chungbok and Malbok. Determined by the lunar calendar, they are thought to be the hottest days of the year. Special rites with offerings of fresh fruits of the season are held to honor one's ancestors and the gods of agriculture on Ch'obok. A bubbling hot soup, usually made of chicken and ginseng, is traditionally eaten on this day as well as on Chungbok and Malbok. Hot chicken and ginseng soup is believed to be an effective panacea to protect against physical weakness during the hottest season of the year. Perhaps the Korean proverb, "Fight heat with heat," comes from this custom.

AUTUMN: SEPTEMBER-OCTOBER

The Siberian high pressure systems begin to form in late September. The dry, cool continental air begins to move in more steadily, bringing clear weather. "High Sky" is the Korean phrase for this condition which brings one of the best seasons of the year. Evenings are cool and the days are pleasant. It is a time for picnics and trips to view the autumn colors in the mountains. It is also one of the most important seasons, for the farmers harvest their crops at this time. Dry and sunny weather is indispensable for rice to ripen and for farmers to reap it. By October the first cold spells are felt at night in the northern area while days remain sunny and dry. For the central and southern parts of Korea this is the season for planting winter crops such as barley and wheat.

Koreans celebrate Ch'usŏk or Harvest Moon, an important holiday determined by the lunar calendar and falling on the 15th day of the eighth month, that is, sometime in late September or early October by the solar calendar. Ch'usŏk is the day of thanksgiving, one of the two biggest holidays in Korea. Each family makes rice cakes and wine and other unusual foods from the newly harvested crops. These foods include such things as sliced bluebell, water lily root, candied walnuts, sun-dried persimmons, honey cakes, chrysanthemum-flavored rice balls and a sweet drink made from rice water flavored with nuts. All members of the family visit the ancestors' graves to offer thanksgiving. For this holiday there are many entertainment activities such as textile weaving contests, cow and tortoise games, tug-of-war games and *Kanggangsuwŏllae*, a traditional round dance.

Kanggangsuwŏllae, *a traditional round dance (above) and* Chajŏnnori, *a chariot fight (right), are among the traditional forms of entertainment enjoyed around* Ch'usŏk, *Korea's "Thanksgiving Day."*

On Sŏl or New Year's Day, families observe ancestral rites (far lower right) and children bow in respect to their parents and older relatives (far upper right).

WINTER: NOVEMBER-MARCH

Winter is dominated by a high pressure system caused by the intense cold over Siberia. The winter season begins in the north in October but in most of Korea the real cold comes later, around January. In December there is little precipitation, though cyclonic storms may bring enough snowfall to provide a snow cover throughout North Korea. During the winter season from January on, the climatic difference between northern and southern Korea is greater. The northern rivers begin to freeze over and the dry, cold air caused by the influence of the Siberian high pressure cell brings severe cold waves, particularly in the north. The temperatures average below freezing during the months of December, January, and February except for the southern coastal areas. The winter in Korea is long, lasting about five months in the northern interior and three months in central and southern Korea. Average temperatures are about −3.5°C (25°F) in Seoul, −2°C (28°F) in Taegu, and 3°C (38°F) in Pusan.

One of the biggest holidays of the year is called Sŏl Day or New Year's Day. It is on the first day of the first lunar month. People dress in their best clothes and all the family gathers together to observe a memorial service to the souls of the ancestors. After the ceremony, formal new year's greetings are said with deep bows to the elders of the family in the order of the grandparents, parents, uncles and aunts. Then children are given a special word of advice and are offered gifts by the elders. After the grand new year's morning meal, young people make a round of visiting relatives and neighbors for further formal greetings. The new year's bows to elder persons are considered essential for the education in good manners and good morals of the young people. The formal new year's greetings to all elders in town continue for ten days. In this way everyone in town can get acquainted with one another very well.

One of the popular new year's games is *yut*. This is similar to a dice game, but, instead of dice, four sticks, almost cylindrical, are used. These are thrown into the air with a twist of the wrist.

The girls play on a see-saw. The Korean way of using a see-saw requires good balance. One girl stands on the end of a long plank and is raised into the air as a companion descends on the opposite end.

Flying kites is another favorite game of the new year's day. Sometimes a contest is held between several kite fliers who cross their strings, coated with powdered glass. After some minutes of pulling and releasing by the pilots on land, the better-maneuvered kite cuts the strings of the weaker.

The new year's festivities last until the 15th day of the month. This is the first full moon of the lunar calendar year. People hike up a nearby hill to greet the first full moon of the year. Whoever sees the moon first is considered the most fortunate, but everyone speaks his wishes to the moon. Ancient Koreans believed that the prayer to the first full moon would have good chances of receiving a favorable answer. One wishes a handsome and beautiful marriage match for the young ones, a son or daughter for the childless couple, and an excellent fall harvest for the farmers. Later in the evening people build big fires and sing and dance all night. This marks the end of the new year festival.

39

Flora

The Rose of Sharon is Korea's national flower.

The climate and differences in temperature and rainfall as already mentioned divide the Korean peninsula into three botanical zones: the northern, central and southern areas.

Many northern plants share common characteristics with those in Manchuria. Generally, alpine plants are found in the north and high mountain areas while the central zones and the western lowlands are dominated by such temperate vegetation as broad-leafed deciduous trees. Such a natural environment makes the land a diversified floral region. An enumeration of Korean plants published by Pak Man-kyu in 1946 listed 201 families, 1,102 genera, 3,347 species, 50 sub-species, 1,012 varieties and 168 formae of higher plants. This means that more than 4,500 kinds of vascular plants grow in Korea. The southern coast and the offshore islands of Chejudo and Ullŭngdo host tropical plants in abundance. Many of the evergreens growing in the southern areas are identical or similar to those in the southwestern part of Japan.

While most of the flora in Korea has common elements with that found in neighboring regions, the peninsula's unique environment has given rise to a few endemic species. For example there are 256 species of evergreens or pines growing throughout the country. The pine tree has a unique natural Oriental beauty wherever it is found. The founder of the Koryŏ Kingdom called his capital city Song-ak, or the pine tree capital. The pine has been a constant in Korean art, and it plays an important part in legend and folklore in general. According to an old Korean saying the pine has four points of beauty: its color, its form, its resistance to lightning, and its perfume. Also pines are very important for wildlife in Korea. Some 50 species of birds and many wild animals eat pine leaves and nuts as their main source of food during the winter season.

Bamboo is the next most important plant. It grows only in the southern provinces, but has become one of the most used in Korean domestic life. From bamboo are made hats, fans, screens, pens, pipes, tub-hoops, paper, flutes, lanterns, bows and a hundred other articles used in Koreans' daily life. Take the bamboo out of Korean painting and half the pictures in the land would be ruined. For its shape it is the symbol of grace, and from its straightness, the regular occurrence of its nodes and its evergreen color, it is the symbol of faithfulness and loyalty. Bamboo is found everywhere, especially at the Confucian shrine. Ancient Koreans planted bamboo as a symbol of loyalty to their king. Incidentally, they believed that loyalty was the ultimate goal of education.

Another noticeable tree is the willow. The mighty row of willows around P'yŏngyang in the north is believed to have been planted by Kija, the second ruler of Chosŏn after Tan-gun, in 1122 B.C. From that time P'yŏngyang city has been known in song and story as "the willow capital." As bamboo is the symbol of faithfulness and loyalty, so the willow is the symbol of peace and womanly beauty. Because of its lightness willow wood is used in making wooden shoes, chests, baskets and other household furniture.

The birch tree is another popular tree throughout the country. One of the hardest woods in Korea comes from birch, which is made into tool handles and especially into laundry boards and clubs. The birch tree (*pakdal*) is mentioned several times in the history of ancient Korea. When

Symbols of faithfulness and loyalty, pine trees and bamboo have been constants in Korean art.

Commelina Communis

Campanula quadricolle

Dicentra Spectabilis

Chrysanthemum indicum

Nelumbo nucifera

Campsis Cohinensis

Cymbidium virescens

Lycoris aurea

Lilium lancifolium

42

Neofinetia falcata

Dianthus superbus

Nymphaea japonokoreana

Platycodon grandiflorum

Chelidonium Sinense

Camellia japonica

Pulsatilla Koreana

Prunella asiatica

Corydalis maximowiczii

43

Hwanung founded the nation it was under the *pakdal* tree. Also when Tan-gun was born it was under the *pakdal* tree. Since then altars have been built with *pakdal* wood. So the birch holds a special place in ancient Korean history.

During the Chosŏn Kingdom the plum tree became the symbol of the country because the founder of the kingdom and its ruling dynasty had the same family name as the name of the plum tree. For this reason plum trees were planted throughout the country from 1392 to 1875.

There are many other hardwood trees found throughout the country such as oak, ginko, elm, and beech. One important to Korean life is the paper-mulberry tree whose inner bark is used for making the tough paper used for the windows, walls, and floors of Korean houses.

Cedar trees are also found in Korea but they are used largely in Buddhist temples as well as for the incense burners of private altars used for ancestral rituals.

There are plenty of fruit trees found throughout the country. Perhaps persimmons take a leading place because they grow to greater perfection in Korea than in any other country. Persimmons grow to the size of an ordinary apple and after the first frost the real delicacy can be tasted. Nowadays persimmon trees are cultivated so that there are sweet persimmons throughout the country. The apricot is another popular fruit, and although it is a little smaller than the Western variety, its flavor is very good. There are many kinds of apples from early summer through fall. Most grow to good size and there are all kinds of flavors. Pears and peaches in Korea are also of the best size and flavor of any found elsewhere in the world. Since labor cost is small in Korea, each apple, pear, and peach grown commercially is wrapped by hand in waxpaper so that they all have protection and keep their good color. Other fruits such as grapes, blackberries, raspberries, cherries and plums are very common in Korea.

As for nuts, one of the most popular is the chestnut. Chestnut trees grow in the mountains throughout the country. Other nuts such as walnuts, pine nuts and gingko nuts are also very common.

This more than 600-year-old juniper on Ullŭngdo Island is a national monument.

Chestnuts

Persimmons

Pine nuts

Jujubes

Gingko nuts

Chinese quince

Walnuts

Apples

45

Fauna

Korea's geographical history, topography, and climate divide the peninsula into highland and lowland areas. Included in the former are the Myohyang Sanmaek Range, the Kaema Plateau and the more rugged terrain of the T'aebaek Sanmaek Range. Most of the highland district lies about 1,046.5 kilometers from Mt. Paektusan along the Korean-Manchurian border.

Animal life in the highland areas is closely similar to that in the arctic zones of Manchuria, mainland China, Siberia, Sakhalin and Hokkaido. Representative species are deer, Manchurian weasel, brown bear, tiger, lynx, northern pika, water shrew, muskrat, ring-necked pheasant, black grouse, hawk owl, pine grosbeak and woodpecker.

The lowland peninsula area has a milder climate and includes the islands of Chejudo and Ullŭngdo. The fauna, closely related to that of southern Manchuria, central China, and Japan, includes black bear, river deer, Manchurian vole, woodpecker, fairy pitta, and ring-necked pheasant.

A common Korean animal is the bullock, which can carry heavy loads, draw carts, and pull ploughs. Until recent times bullocks carried out all the heavy duties of Korean agriculture.

The Korean pony is unique, at least in Eastern Asia. It is a little larger than the Shetland pony, and it is not commonly used for ploughing or drawing carts, but is used often for the traveller who packs a huge bundle onto the pony. It is so tough that it can carry more than half its

The Naktonggang River Delta in Kyŏngsangnam-do is a stopover for a variety of migratory birds.

own weight a distance of 48 kilometers in a day.

The donkey is another popular animal which was formerly used for pulling carts and for travelling. Even though it can not carry a very heavy load like the bullock, it can go much faster.

Among the wild beasts the tiger is a leading animal though its numbers are dwindling at the present time. This species was once distributed throughout the country. Many tigers were captured in all parts of Korea prior to World War II. It is believed that any surviving Korean tigers make the rugged terrain of Mt. Paektusan, North Korea, their habitat.

Deer are common throughout the land. They are mostly river deer and are darker brown in color than the Chinese river deer. In springtime they are eagerly sought for their soft horns which are considered to be of great medicinal value. The bear is found occasionally but is of a small breed. The wild boar, while not very abundant, is a formidable animal because it will charge an enemy at sight.

The fox is found in every rural area in the country. It is the most detested animal of all. The land is full of stories of evil people who turned out to be foxes in human guise.

Among the less abundant animals are the badger, hedgehog, squirrel, wildcat, otter, weasel, leopard, lynx, wolf, marten, roe deer and amur goral. A few species such as bat, shrew, striped hamster, and muskrat are found only in North Korea. Other species of wildlife in South Korea include 25 kinds of reptiles, 14 kinds of amphibians, and 130 kinds of freshwater fish.

Some 370 species of birds have been recorded in South Korea. About 48 of them are permanent residents and 266 species are migrants. One of the most popular game birds is the ring-neck pheasant, which is found everywhere in Korea. It stands about 1.2 meters high and weighs, when dressed, from 9 to 13.5 kilograms. It is much like the wild turkey. Ducks of a dozen varieties, geese, swans, and other aquatic birds are found in winter. Quail, snipe and other small birds are plentiful everywhere. Various kinds of storks, cranes, herons, and hawks are found throughout the country, too.

The tortoise is plentiful in Korea, and it plays an important part in Korean legend and fairy tales. It represents to the Korean mind the principle of healthy conservation. It is never in a hurry, thinking things through; perhaps this is why Koreans look upon it with such respect, if not affection.

One big factor in the Korean diet is that fish are plentiful throughout Korea. Hundreds of kinds of fish live and thrive in the waters of Korea's many rivers and surrounding seas. Almost all varieties are eaten by the people, even the sharks and the octopuses. Various kinds of clams, oysters, and shrimp are common. Pearl oysters are found in large numbers along the southern coast. Fish and pearls are not the only sea products that Koreans use. Enormous quantities of all kinds of edible seaweed are gathered and prepared for Korean dishes.

Twenty-three species of wildlife have been designated as protected species and 20 birds, two mammals, and several insect species are designated as endangered species. Included among these species are the white-bellied black woodpecker, Japanese crested ibis, white stork, black stork, whooper Manchurian crane, white-naped crane, fairy pitta, black-faced spoonbill, great bustard, Japanese wood pigeon, musk deer, Amur goral, long-horned bettle, hooded crane, black woodpecker, black vulture, Steller's sea eagle, white-tailed eagle and golden eagle.

White-bellied Black Woodpecker

Goshawk

Golden Eagle

Mandarin Duck

Manchurian Crane

White-naped Crane

Upupa epops saturata

Japanese Crested Ibis

49

Part Two
Cultural and Political Heritage

The Beginning of Korea

Many national myths attempt to explain the origin of human civilization and the origin of particular nations' social customs and ways of life. By examining myths of various cultures one can better understand how these cultures differ and how they resemble one another. Koreans have a myth to explain the origin of their own civilization. It goes something like this.

Long, long ago when heaven and earth were one and when animals could speak like humans, there lived a god whose name was Hwanin. He governed the eastern part of the world, the land from whence the morning comes.

Hwanin had a son, Hwanung, who was a young man possessed with wisdom, honor, bravery, power, and trustworthiness. Hwanin loved his son very much.

One day Hwanin called his son to him and inquired, "Have you heard of the eastern land?"

"Yes, Father, the inhabitants of that land are known to be gentle and humble," replied Hwanung.

"I am interested in sending you to the eastern land to build a new country there," Hwanin informed him.

After considering this idea for a little while Hwanung answered his father. "If this is your wish, I shall try to fulfill your desire, Father." Hwanin had great confidence in his son and foresaw that one day Hwanung would be a great ruler for the eastern land.

Thus it came about that Hwanung descended from heaven to the east with three divine spirits, namely the wind-general, the rain-governor, and the cloud-teacher. Accompanying them were 3,000 other spirits who appeared on T'aebaeksan Mountain, which is near the city of P'yŏngyang, the current capital of North Korea.

Hwanung gathered with his followers on Mt. T'aebaeksan under the shade of an ancient birch tree. It was in the 25th year of the Emperor Yao in China, which corresponds to the year 2333 B.C. Hwanung governed this country through his three vice-regents, the wind-general, the rain-governor, and the cloud-teacher. They lived happily, and the city where they lived was designated Shinshi, which means "divine city."

Not far from Shinshi in a small cave there lived a bear and a tiger. One day as they sat together on the mountainside the bear mused to the tiger. "How I wish we could live like men!" To this the tiger responded, "Do you imagine there is any way at all by which we *could* become men?"

Since Hwanung had begun governing the country all its inhabitants lived happily. Thus the bear and the tiger had become envious of men there. Now they both wished they could become men too. The bear and the tiger dreamed and wished. One day they decided to go to see Hwanung. When they arrived they eagerly told Hwanung of their wishes. "We both wish to become men. Could you help us?"

To their pleading the kind king Hwanung responded, "Yes, there is a way. But it is very difficult."

"We are willing to try no matter how difficult it is," the bear and the tiger anxiously replied.

"It will require great patience of you," warned Hwanung.

"We believe that we possess enough patience," both the bear and the

Tan-gun, the legendary founder of the Korean nation (right), in whose honor a ceremony is held annually on National Foundation Day, October 3, atop Mt. Manisan on Kanghwado Island (below).

tiger eagerly replied.

After some thought and preparation Hwanung gave them their instructions with his blessing. "Here are 20 garlic cloves and some artemisia for you both. Eat them and stay secluded in your cave for 100 days without sunlight. If you will pray earnestly, then you will become men."

The bear and the tiger proceeded to carry out Hwanung's instructions. They went into their cave, ate the garlic cloves and the artemisia and began praying. To eat the spices was no hardship but for them to remain all the time inside the cave began to become quite burdensome. Being wild animals, they were accustomed to roaming freely around the mountain. So it became harder as time went on for them to endure. But they thought again of their objective to become men and so they endeavored to be patient.

After about 20 days had passed, the tiger was nearing the end of his patience. "I have had almost all I can endure. If I wait 80 more days, I shall have starved to death anyway," he reasoned. He felt very bad, he

Dolmen (left) are one of the predominant forms of burial that survive from the Bronze Age. At right (clockwise from top): stone daggers, 10th century B.C.; a comb-pattern pottery jar, Neolithic Age, 3000-2000 B.C.; and a Neolithic dwelling site in Amsa-dong, Seoul.

looked bad, and his eyes were hardly able to focus.

"Listen, bear, I am almost gone. Let us go out and make an end of this vigil," the hungry tiger pleaded.

"No, we were warned that it would not be easy to become men. Try to concentrate on the goal and not to think of being hungry," encouraged the bear.

But after a while the tiger gave up. "I have had enough of this waiting. I am getting out. I don't care about becoming a man after all." With those words the tiger limped out of the cave to find food.

It was a great temptation to the bear to leave. But he reminded himself again of his desire to become a man, and he began to pray all the more. So the bear, with greater patience than the tiger, endured his hardships.

When the hundred days were almost passed, the bear's body began to change. It started to lose its hair and the back feet were being transformed into a shape like human feet.

At last, at the end of the hundredth day, the bear became a beautiful

maiden.

"Finally, I have become a person! I am so happy!" the bear-girl said. She looked toward heaven and offered thanks to the deities. Then she went to thank Hwanung for his blessing. When she came out into the fresh air and sunshine, she appeared even more beautiful.

Hwanung was amazed when he saw her. She was the most beautiful girl he had ever seen. "I am the one incarnated from the bear with your blessing. I wish I could repay your kindness somehow," she told him.

Hwanung considered that she needed a name, so he called her "Ung-yŏ" which means "the girl incarnated from a bear." Ung-yŏ seemed to grow more beautiful each day and she was clearly distinguished from all the other maidens. After a while Hwanung proposed to Ung-yŏ and she consented to their marriage. From their union a son was born, who was given the name Tan-gun which alternately means "Lord of the Birch Trees" or "Medicine Man."

After becoming a man Tan-gun united the six tribes in the northern part of Korea and set up the first nation there. They named their nation "Chosŏn" which means the "Land of Morning Calm," and P'yŏngyang was chosen as the capital city.

Tan-gun taught his people about government, marriage, agriculture, cooking, housing and all aspects of life. He ruled the nation of Chosŏn until 1122 B.C.

This myth, which may seem irrational and inconsistent to the scientifically-minded modern man, represents the whole foundation of Korean culture. The truth of this myth was unquestioned by the ancient Chosŏn people, because it was so closely associated with their sacred beliefs.

First of all, Tan-gun was believed to have been born with divine, supernatural powers greater than those of any mere human being, and to possess human characteristics. In the Tan-gun myth, Hwanung descended from heaven to the earth with three divine spirits, namely the wind-general, the rain-governor, and the cloud teacher. In an early agricultural society the greatest dangers were famine and natural disasters. Since man could not control the rain and the wind, he worshiped the gods who supposedly controlled these things. The Ancient Chosŏn people thought the greatest dangers to a man's life was to offend heaven and to have no rainfall. Therefore, the fact that Hwanung brought these most important wind and rain gods with him caused them to make him their absolute ruler.

Secondly, the people of the northern areas, like eastern Siberia, Manchuria and Mongolia from which areas the Koreans migrated, considered bears as unique and superior creatures, powerful and respected above all other animals.

Connecting the two theories above, other archaeological excavations, legendary sources, and linguistic studies agree that Altaic speaking tribes in the regions of northern China and eastern Siberia migrated to the east. Ethnologically they belong to the races which includes the Turkish, Mongolian and Tungusic people. They eventually became known as Koreans, who formed a homogeneous race sharing distinct physical characteristics, one language, and one culture. All primitive people revered their legends and regarded the transmission of them to succeeding generations as a solemn duty. This attitude has been particularly manifested in nations consisting of a single race. As mentioned earlier Choson means the "Land of Morning Calm," touched

Bronze finial with jingles excavated from a site in Kangwon-do, Late Bronze or Early Iron Age, 3rd-2nd century B.C.

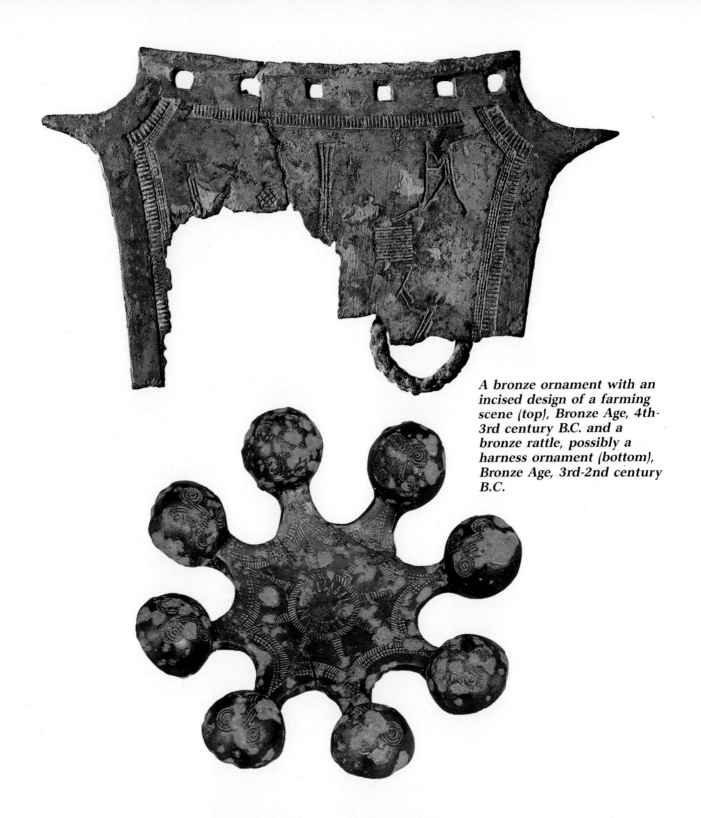

A bronze ornament with an incised design of a farming scene (top), Bronze Age, 4th-3rd century B.C. and a bronze rattle, possibly a harness ornament (bottom), Bronze Age, 3rd-2nd century B.C.

by the first beams of the rising sun. There is a trend among many primitive peoples to name their lands with words related to the sun.

The Koreans' love of white clothes may date back to this age too. White has always been a symbol of brightness stemming from a deep-rooted religious belief. The sun-worshipers loved and respected white, and in their religious ceremonies it was regarded as the most sacred color.

Excavations of a few of the hundreds of ancient burial sites on the Korean peninsula indicate advanced civilizations existed during this era. Un-earthed items include excellent examples of pottery, jewelry, battle equipment, bronze mirrors and bells.

The Three Kingdoms (57 B.C.-A.D. 935)

Historical Background

This is the first period in the recorded history of Korea described in the monumental work called *Samguksagi* (The History of the Three Kingdoms) which was completed by Kim Pushik in 1145. The Tan-gun Chosŏn lasted 1,200 years, followed by the Kija Chosŏn era of about 99 years. Later Kija Chosŏn was split into various tribal states. Among these tribal states, Koguryŏ (37 B.C.-A.D. 668) was the first to found a kingdom. The nation occupied the whole of Manchuria, the Yalu River basin, and the northern part of the Korean peninsula. Next came the Kingdom of Paekche (18 B.C.-A.D. 660) which was located in the western part of the southern portion of present-day Korea. The third and last kingdom was the Shilla Kingdom, (57 B.C.-A.D. 935) centered on the southeast part of Korea with its capital at Kyŏngju.

Even though all three kingdoms were established by various members of the same race, they all were founded in different times and in different locations. They also developed in different directions in economics and in foreign relations. The three kingdoms became more civilized and developed state government organization, taking over the Confucian and Buddhist hierarchical structures and establishing royal hereditary systems. Each of the three kingdoms also began to compile its history. These three kingdoms competed with each other in strength as they waged war with one another periodically over a period of 700 years. The Shilla Kingdom also suffered a great deal from raids by pirates from Japan. However, the Shilla Kingdom, with the help of China, unified with Paekche in 660 A.D. and with Koguryŏ in 668.

Korea at the height of Koguryŏ expansion in the 5th century

Koguryŏ

• P'yŏngyang

Ungjin (Kongju) **Shilla**

Sabi (Puyŏ)

Kŭmsŏng (Kyŏngj

Kaya

Paekche

Chejudo Island

Hunting scene from the west wall of the burial chamber of the Tomb of Dancers, Koguryŏ, late 5th-early 6th century.

58

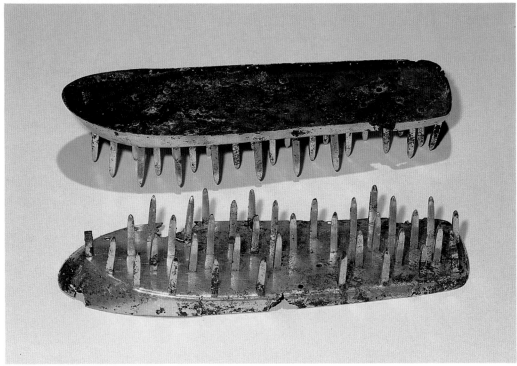

*Gilt bronze phoenix
ornaments (above)
and shoes (left)
of Koguryŏ origin.*

59

Seventh century stoneware and earthenware tiles (left) of Paekche origin excavated from a site in Puyŏ, a capital of the Paekche Kingdom; 5th-6th century stoneware vessels (below) of Kaya origin excavated from a site in the Kyŏngsang-do area; and glass beads, jade commas and other pieces of jewelry excavated from the tomb of Paekche's King Muryŏng-wang (r. 501-523) in Kongju (right).

Cultural Background

As the stone age is the cultural background of Tan-gun and Kija Chosŏn, the bronze and metal age was the beginning of culture in the period of the Three Kingdoms. This is evidenced by the royal tombs which have been excavated to reveal many beautiful crowns, buckles, and other ornaments of soft gold, in some cases decorated with jade and colored glass.

During the Three Kingdoms period, one of the most significant cultural developments was the introduction of Buddhism and Confucianism. Koguryŏ was the first to adopt Buddhism as a royal creed in 372, Paekche the second in 384, and Shilla the last in 528.

Buddhism not only brought a civilizing force to the wild tribes, but reformed the spiritual life of the early Koreans. Furthermore Buddhism gave to the people of the three kingdoms a new vision in the world of

The Unfied Shilla and Parhae Kingdoms (8th century)

Sanggyŏng

Parhae

Unified Shilla

Kŭmsŏng (Kyŏngju)

Chejudo Island

art. They built many monasteries with stupendous architectural ability. From this influence came paintings in tombs, statues in temples, other paintings, and pagodas which are altogether some of the most beautiful examples of the fine arts. One of the temples built during the era is Pulguksa made during the reign of King Pŏphŭng (r. 514-540). Pulguksa, "Temple of the Buddha Land," is one of the most famous, splendid examples of the Shilla-era architecture still existing today in Kyŏngju. Shilla also fostered science, as evidenced by a stone observatory, Ch'ŏmsŏngdae, which was built in 647. It is probably the oldest of the observatories still remaining in East Asia.

With the overall growth of culture, one of the most impressive developments in the Shilla Kingdom was the *Hwarangdo,* a unique system of training young men. Handsome and intelligent young men from upper class families were selected for this school, which was similar to a fraternity of knighthood. The *Hwarangdo* (Flower of Youth Corps) students received an education that consisted of fostering academic and military skills. In fact nearly equal emphasis was placed on the study of Chinese classics, history, philosophy, religion and the teaching of various forms of warlike techniques. Men of virtue and intellect were often selected from this group to serve the government as statesmen and military leaders.

The guiding principles of the *Hwarang* were loyalty, filial duty, trust-worthiness, valor and justice. The objectives were postulated by the famous priest, Won-gwang, who consolidated Buddhist-Confucian virtues in the education of youths. Members of the *Hwarang* also made a practice of visiting places of scenic beauty to develop a sense of appreciation of natural phenomenon and broad-mindedness; they also learned to write poems and music and to recite poetry when they visited scenic places.

A spirit of chivalry and patriotism resulted from such education. In time

of war *Hwarang* members fought valiantly on the battlefield. General Kim Yushin, who played a key role in Shilla's unification of the three kingdoms, was a graduate of the youth corps.

Some of the most interesting features of the *Hwarangdo* schools were their five commandments which stressed the virtues of filial piety and loyalty to the king derived from Confucian teaching, as well as restraint on unnecessary taking of life and other points of justice taken from Buddhism. The *Hwarangdo* teachers developed concepts that would har-monize beliefs taken from Buddhism, Confucianism, Taoism and the other native religions; they had to create a new curriculum for teaching the *Hwarang.* Thus, the *Hwarangdo* school inculcated a spirit of harmony and unity in the youths and, in turn, expressed itself in flexible approaches to society. This very idea of harmony or unity became the foundation for unification of the three kingdoms when once again Tan-gun's Chosŏn people were united under one nation.

Pulguksa Temple in Kyŏngju (far left). A modern depiction of some members of Shilla's **Hwarangdo** *or "Flower of Youth Corps" (above).*

64

Glass vessels of Shilla origin, harness accessories of Kaya origin, some column bases excavated at the site of the 7th century Hwangnyŏngsa Temple in Kyŏngju, a boundary marker erected by Shilla's King Chinhŭng, and a pottery vessel excavated from a Shilla tomb (counterclockwise from left).

The Koryŏ Kingdom (918-1392)

Historical Background

A golden age followed the unification of Korea in the Shilla period, which also marked the beginning of a long process of solidification of the Korean people as a distinct nation, with their own unique culture. For more than 230 years the Shilla Kingdom enjoyed peace resulting from national unity and from friendly relations with T'ang China. There was no longer a struggle among the Korean people themselves and peaceful intercourse with other Asian nations served to encourage the productive efforts of the Koreans, who attained a high peak of cultural achievement during the Shilla era.

However, toward the end of the kingdom the ruling class grew extremely decadent, completely ignoring the welfare of the people and the nation as a whole. The brilliance of the cultural achievements contrasted with the misery and hardship of the common people. Historical records show that at least 78 open revolts took place during the last decades of that era, as the northern provinces took form.

These insurgent elements finally united under a great leader, General Wang Kŏn, who founded the Koryŏ Kingdom in 918. Koryŏ did not attack Shilla but awaited its downfall through self-destruction. In 935 the last king of Shilla finally surrendered peacefully.

The establishment of Koryŏ and its takeover of the country had two far-reaching effects. First, it not only saved the nation from disintegration but also enabled the Koreans to defend their territory from the tribes in the northern part of Korea. Koryŏ consolidated territorial unity by completely subjugating minor dissidents in the northern provinces, while at the same time stationing a strong defense force along the northern boundary to repel invaders. Further, Koryŏ occupied a much more strategic position than its predecessors in dealing with the northern defense problems, for its capital was in Song-ak, which is located in the central part of the country.

The new kingdom was not only diligent in national defense, but during the early days made great advances in all fields of government. The Koryŏ government installed a civil service examination system to recruit officials by merit. Farmlands were reorganized, each farmer being given a certain plot of land during his lifetime. Further, various social security measures were introduced and educational facilities were greatly expanded.

For the next 200 years Koryŏ enjoyed peace, until early in the 13th century when the Mongolian invasion came. The Mongols, rising from the remote interior of Mongolia, had become a great power under Genghis Khan, conquering most of the nations on the Asian continent one after another. In 1225 the mongols emerged victorious over the Ch'in Empire in China and then began to apply military pressure on Koryŏ. In 1231, the Mongol hordes attacked Koryŏ but they could not overwhelm Koryŏ entirely. As the devastating and futile peninsular war dragged out for 40 years, the Mongols finally offered to make peace. For the next hundred years peace was generally kept, although the psychological hostility of the Koreans toward the Mongols long persisted, together with resentment and contempt toward them and a deep pride that Koryŏ had been the only Asian nation to successfully resist the Mongol invasion.

66

A modern depiction of Koryŏ's General Kang Kamch'an repulsing Mongolian invaders.

The Koryŏ Kingdom
(8th century)

Sŏgyŏng (P'yŏngyang)

Kaegyŏng (Kaesŏng)

Namgyŏng (Seoul)

Tonggyŏng

Chejudo Island

Cultural Background

During the Koryŏ Kingdom, Korea's widespread and active foreign trade and communications stimulated a veritable flood of cultural development within the peninsula. At the beginning of the Koryŏ Kingdom the Korean people were already famous for excellent ceramics which far surpassed the finest Chinese works of the Sung Dynasty. In particular, Koryŏ's jade blue celadon porcelain won the admiration of the world. Some relics later reached various European nations and America, where their classical perfection of lines and color attained for them an unchallenged reputation

An inlaid celadon maebyŏng vase (right), a dragon shaped celadon vessel with incised design (lower left) and a tortoise shaped celadon wine vessel with incised design (lower right), all of Koryŏ origin and dating from the 12th century.

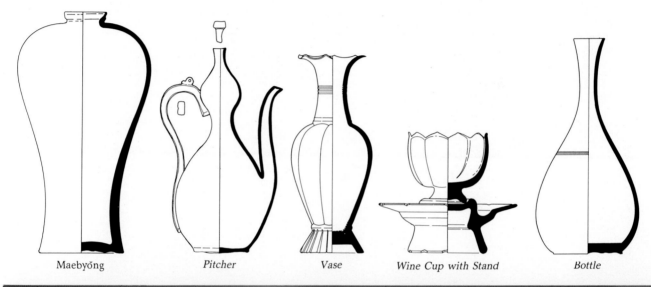

Maebyŏng   Pitcher   Vase   Wine Cup with Stand   Bottle

as artistic works of the highest standard.

One of the greatest cultural legacies of this kingdom was the work of collecting, engraving, and publishing of the *Tripitaka Koreana* or Buddhist sutras. The occasion of and motive for the enterprise was the Mongol invasion. When the Mongols invaded Korea, the government was moved from Kaesŏng to an island fortress off the central west coast of Korea. There, a court of devoted Buddhists, believing in the power of prayer to Buddha, undertook to engrave the best text of all Buddhist scriptures as a form of prayer to expel the invaders. It took 16 years to engrave the 80,000 wooden plates of the *Tripitaka*. This work has been preserved intact and is now kept in Haeinsa Temple in South Korea. It is in fact the oldest, most accurate and complete sutras of Mahayana Buddhism.

Movable metal type is reputed to be one of the greatest inventions of the Koryŏ people. In 1234 a number of voluminous books were printed with movable metal type. Although a German inventor, Gutenberg, is credited in the West with designing lead-cast printing type in 1450, the metal type of Koryŏ actually preceded it by some 220 years. As time passed printing type was improved. Later, during the Chosŏn Kingdom, the royal government sponsored, on almost 20 separate occasions, the production of printing types made of copper. Many of these copper types of Korean origin, along with the techniques of producing them, were subsequently introduced into China and Japan.

The wood blocks used to print the Tripitaka Koreana, carved between 1237 and 1252 (above), are preserved in ideal conditions in a naturally ventilated storehouse (opposite) at Haeinsa Temple. Movable metal type, one of the greatest inventions of the Koryŏ people.

One of the special features of Koryŏ architecture was the abundant use of granite in the construction of the steps and foundations of temples, palaces, and royal tombs. The best specimen is King Kongmin's Tomb where the king and his queen were buried in a granite chamber 90 square meters, covered with a grassy mound and enclosed with granite foundation circles and granite railings, attended by lions, tigers, and goats, all carved in granite. Stone pagodas were erected in hexagonal or octagonal forms during the middle period of the kingdom. The seven-story pagoda of the Hyŏnhwasa Temple, erected along with an ornamental stone lamp in the environs of Kaesŏng, is a representative masterpiece in its magnitude and beauty of detail. A stone lantern and a standing image of Buddha at Kwanch'oksa Temple are great Koryŏ sculptures. The giant stone image of Maitreya Buddha was carved of two massive pieces of granite more than 15.3 meters in height. Taking 38 years to complete, this gigantic but lifelike artwork is a marvel of Koryŏ.

Also during this era Korea was introduced to the West for the first time by the Venetian merchant, Marco Polo, who made a journey through China about 1260. When he got back to Venice in 1295, Polo gave an account of his experience. At that time, Koryŏ carried on traffic with the Mongols to and from Peking, and perhaps it was Marco Polo who introduced Koryŏ to the Western world as "Coree," "Corea," or "Korea."

The interior of the Muryang-sujŏn Hall of Pusŏksa Temple which, constructed in 1376, is one of the oldest wooden structures in Korea (below). A large stone lantern and image of Maitreya, the Buddha of the Future, at Kwanch'oksa Temple in Nonsan (right).

The Chosŏn Kingdom (1392-1910)

Historical Background

The Chosŏn Kingdom (15th century)

Hamhŭng
P'yŏngyang
Haeju
Hansŏng (Seoul)
Wŏnju
Kongju
Taegu
Kyŏngju
Chŏnju

Chejudo Island

A Chosŏn period folding screen with a painting showing the layout of Ch'angdŏkkung Palace (opposite page).

From its beginning the Koryŏ government was greatly influenced by the Buddhist priesthood which gradually encroached on the rights of state and assumed more and more political power. The Buddhist cult eventually attained such power that it was necessary for the king to become a Buddhist monk to reign. The last of the Koryŏ kings, controlled by a scheming Buddhist monk, was goaded into attacking the powerful Chinese forces of the Ming Dynasty. Against universal opposition and in violation of the long-standing Korean practice of not invading its neighbors, the king insisted on attacking China. He ordered his general, Yi Sŏng-gye, to lead the army to the Yalu and to invade Manchuria. General Yi, who was one of the most brilliant and influential military leaders, backed by the almost unanimous support of the people, revolted. Laying siege to the capital with his army, he sent an ultimatum to the king, and when the king refused to concede, General Yi ordered his troops to capture the palace and take over the capital. The Koryŏ king was thus ousted and General Yi was installed as the first monarch of a new kingdom, Chosŏn.

The Chosŏn Kingdom, which moved the capital from Song-ak to Hanyang (Seoul), promptly introduced many reforms which improved the economic life of the common people and allowed them to submit petitions to the government. Various beneficial laws resulted from the reforms: for example, the government installed in 1402 the "Drum of Appeal," which was hung upon the tower of the king's palace in Seoul and in the chief centers throughout the country for any oppressed persons to beat so that justice might be given. The basic principle of the new kingdom was Confucianism, in place of Buddhism, which had been dominant in Koryŏ. The Chosŏn monarchs vigorously supressed Buddhism. Lands owned by Buddhist temples were redistributed to farmers.

During the first one hundred years of its rule, the Chosŏn Kingdom made an interesting political and military change. While Koryŏ had been a Buddhist state under the dominant power of military leaders, the Yi Dynasty's Chosŏn was a kingdom ruled by civilians who faithfully followed the Confucian principles.

The cultural growth and social development of the early days, however, was followed by foreign invasion, as was the case during the Koryŏ Kingdom. Toward the end of the 16th century, Japan became a military power under a warlord, Toyotomi Hideyoshi who unified all the contending military groups in the islands of Japan. The Japanese grew in strength of attacking Ming China,, with which they were not on good terms. of attackisng the Ming China, with which they were not on good terms. The Japanese saw Korea as a bridge to the Chinese mainland and determined to march up the Korean peninsula. Hideyoshi sent a number of envoys to the Korean king proposing that the two nations enter into an alliance to crush China, but the Korean ruler declined, saying that his nation had been friendly with China for centuries. The Japanese thereupon determined to resort to war to gain their path across Korea.

In 1592, Hideyoshi's 200,000 men, assisted by a large fleet, landed on Korea's southern coast and headed north. Having spent two centuries in peace and in cultural rather than military activities, the Korean defenders

were at an extreme disadvantage. They lacked troops as well as adequate weapons. The Korean ground troops were equipped with bows and arrows, while the Japanese warriors were armed with shotguns and long spears.

The Japanese invading forces made rapid progress, but were soon confronted by the strong resistance of local volunteers and hastily organized private resistance groups which forced the Japanese to come to a gradual halt. With the very existence of Korea thus at stake, there emerged a great national hero, Admiral Yi Sun-shin. Admiral Yi was a genius in naval tactics and succeeded by using a highly effective warship of his own design; the *Kŏbuksŏn* or turtle warship.

This was a big boat 2.16 meters high, 20.7 meters long, with a topmast 34.4 meters high and with no keel but with a flat bottom made of ten heavy boards. On its back were driven iron spikes, like sharp, reversed sabers, to pierce the feet of any enemy jumping onto it. The only opening was a narrow passage in the shape of a cross on the surface for its own crew to traverse freely. All important parts of the hull were covered with protective iron. Mounted on the bow or the turtle's head, which they called the Dragon Head, were four guns that threw flames of sulphur and gunpowder while spreading a smokescreen all around the boat. A turret on the stern formed the turtle's tail. There were six gun ports on the lower deck, port and seaboard, and 22 gunholes on the upper deck, while a flag, bearing an image of a tutle flew at the mast. When engaging the wooden enemy vessels in battle, the turtle's upper deck was covered with straw mats for camouflage, and it swiftly rode the waves as its cannon balls and fire-arrows sent destruction to the enemy targets.

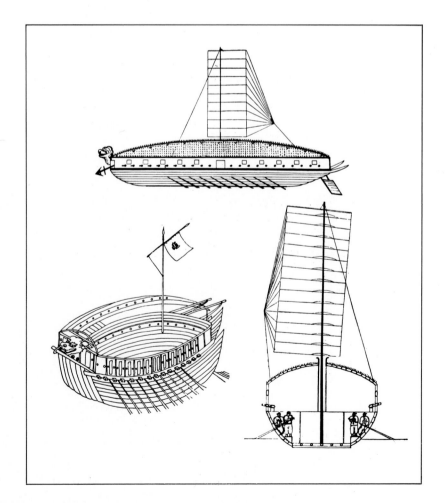

A modern depiction of Admiral Yi Sun-shin directing the construction of a turtle warship (right). At left are some drawings of some warship designs.

A screen with a painting showing a fleet of warships under the command of Admiral Yi Sun-shin that harassed Japanese invaders off the southern coast during the 1592-98 Japanese invasions (right). Hyŏnch'ungsa, a shrine to admiral Yi located at his birthplace in Asan, Ch'ungch'ŏngnam-do (below).

There were ten oars on each side of the boat, which enabled it to outrun the enemy vessels. Since it was constructed on the order of a turtle, its own sailors could look out from inside, but the enemy could not look in from outside. The whole frame was armored with double iron plates and iron railings, making it almost impregnable. This turtle warship was the first ironclad warship in history.

First Admiral Yi sailed against the Japanese fleet and destroyed it. Next he exterminated an enemy fleet reinforcement off Hansando Island. His triumphs completely frustrated the enemy strategy, which was to make parallel advances both on land and on sea. Moreover, the entire Japanese position was threatened, for Admiral Yi was then able to command the sea and to cut off the enemy's supply of ammunition and food. Admiral Yi's force destroyed almost the entire fleet Japan had sent to Korea. At the same time, Korean patriots rose in all parts of the country and defeated the Japanese army in many guerrilla battles. The Japanese troops were finally driven out of Korea in 1598. As they sailed for home their rebuilt fleet was again set upon by Admiral Yi. The entire fleet was destroyed for the third time, but Admiral Yi was mortally wounded during the engagement. His death, however, was kept secret by his order until the Korean fleet had completed the resounding victory over the fleeing Japanese all along the southern coast of Korea.

The outcome of the war, which had lasted for seven years, was very significant for Korea. For the first time Koreans felt a sense of nationalism, which was developed through united resistance against the alien invaders.

78

Cultural Background

The Chosŏn Kingdom, from the close of the 14th century to recent times, marked the beginning of the modern age of Korea. Shortly after the foundation of the new Kingdom of Chosŏn, in 1398, King T'aejo opened Sŏnggyun-gwan, which was an institution of higher learning. This institution was established for the purpose of training the nation's future leaders. The first class was made up of 150 students who had successfully passed the first examination for the government service, and the first faculty of 26 professors was appointed by the king. Admission to Sŏnggyun-wan was restricted to boys from the ruling *yangban* class. Every student was required to reside in the dormitory on the campus, and their schooling and boarding expenses were fully paid for by the government. As Sŏng, means "perfecting human nature," *gyun* means "building a harmonious society", and *gwan* means "institution," the name of this higher learning institution explained the objectives of this school as an institution for building a harmonious society of perfected human beings. The curriculum for this institution consisted of manners, music, archery, horseriding, the Chinese classics (literature) and mathematics.

Now Sŏnggyun-gwan University, with 588 years of history, has grown to become one of the major universities in Korea. The university is now made up of 11 colleges, five postgraduate schools and four professional graduate schools.

Munmyo, the nation's main Confucian shrine, on the premises of Sŏnggyun-gwan University in Seoul (left). Tosan Sŏwon, a Confucian shrine-academy in Andong, Kyŏngsangbuk-do (above) and some ancient books on the thought of Yi Hwang (T'oegye, 1501-70), one of Chosŏn's foremost Confucian scholars (right).

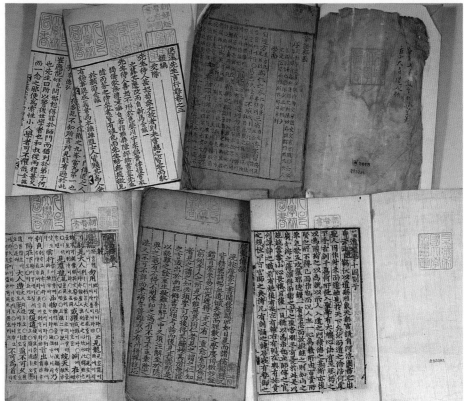

A sundial (right), a rain gauge (below) and a water clock (opposite) produced during the reign of Chosŏn's King Sejong (r. 1418-50).

The cultural growth, which started with great vigor from the inception of the Chosŏn Kingdom, reached the highest peak during the reign of King Sejong in the 15th century. King Sejong, the fourth monarch of the Chosŏn Kingdom, was a ruler unequalled in Korean history. He left behind a record of achievements in many fields, especially in literature, science and the fine arts. He was a Korean Leonardo da Vinci in the variety and magnitude of his gifts. Among the many astronomical instruments he invented, a water clock (chagyŏngnu), is the best known and most admired. Unlike other timekeepers of crude construction, this water clock was an intricate and elaborate instrument.

Using water as it motive power, *chagyŏngnu* was so constructed as to indicate automatically not only the time of day, but also such astronomical phenomena as changes of seasons, the varying times of sunrise and sunset, and similar data pertaining to the moon. In its operation the water clock made use of a number of wooden pieces, one for the time of day, another for the time of sunrise, and so on.

Another of the many instruments created under the personal direction of Sejong was the rain gauge. Like many Oriental rulers King Sejong was very much interested in the development of agriculture. In 1423 he started to think about a device to measure the amount of rainfall that had seeped into the ground. In 1441 he succeeded in produing a number of rain gauges of uniform size and standard capabilities. He also adopted a standard unit of measurement to be used with the rain gauges. These instruments were then distributed to local government agencies, and officials were charged with the responsibility of measuirng and recording each rainfall. The results were reported to the central government of King Sejong and upon compilation they served as an important basis for fairly accurate crop forecasts in the various parts of the country.

But by far the greatest contribution to Korean cultural development made by King Sejong was his invention of the Korean alphabet. Originally known as *hunmin-chŏngŭm* which means "proper-sounds to instruct the people," the Korean alphabet later came to be known as *Han-gŭl.* Its invention is perhaps the most brilliant achievement throughout the history of Korean culture in view of its scientific efficiency and its excellent usefulness as a system of phonetic symbols. Since the use of Chinese characters had been well established for centuries among educated Koreans, no serious consideration had been paid by the people to the formation of their own alphabet. King Sejong, however, wishing to end illiteracy among the general public, determined to create an easy-to-learn, simple, Korean alphabet.

As invented by King Sejong, the alphabet consisted of 17 consonants and 11 vowels, 28 letters in all. As the language has developed, now the Korean alphabet consists of 10 vowels and 14 consonants which are combined to form syllables. These 24 letters offer an almost unlimited possibility of combination and interchange, thereby completely indicating all Korean vocal sounds. The shape of each letter is a simple geometric design.

Han-gŭl has a system whereby sounds can be expressed and combinations of letters effected in a completely scientific way. It is not only the most recent of the world's alphabets but also the most complete system of phonetic letters ever invented.

Unlike Chinese characters, there is no semantic symbolism involved in *Han-gŭl.* A Korean syllable consists of three elements, initial consonant, middle vowel, and closing consonant. A syllable cannot be written without a vowel, and so the middle vowel is indispensable in a syllable, while on the other hand, a syllable may have both, neither, or either, of the two consonants (initial and closing).

Another epochal achievement of King Sejong was the comprehensive accumulation and organization of medical knowledge of his day into an encyclopedia entitled *Ŭibang Yuch'wi,* a work of 365 volumes, finished in 1445. The Chinese have recently used this encyclopedia to recover some of their own medical information lost in the war with Japan.

Modern paintings showing King Sejong and his crown prince observing the North Star in a garden in Kyŏngbokkung Palace, the printing of books with improved metal type during Sejong's reign, and Pak Yŏn, a music scholar Sejong ordered to rearrange music scores and develop musical instruments, demonstrating a set of stone chimes for the King.

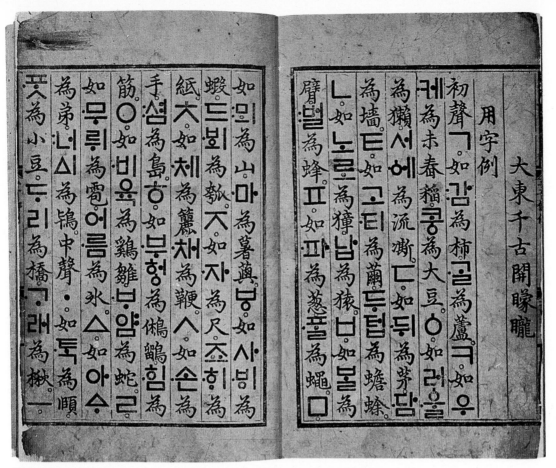

Hunmin-chŏngŭm, *"proper sounds to instruct the people,"* illustrating the pronunciation of the letters of the Han-gŭl alphabet.

The Korean Alphabet

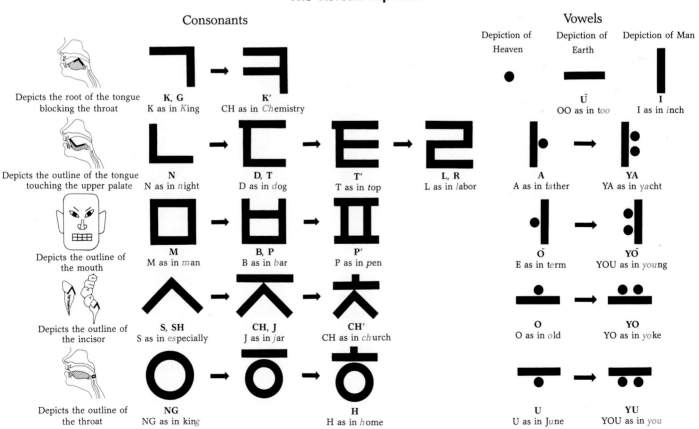

Consonants					Vowels	

Depicts the root of the tongue blocking the throat

K, G — K as in King → **K'** — CH as in Chemistry

Depicts the outline of the tongue touching the upper palate

N — N as in night → **D, T** — D as in dog → **T'** — T as in top → **L, R** — L as in labor

Depicts the outline of the mouth

M — M as in man → **B, P** — B as in bar → **P'** — P as in pen

Depicts the outline of the incisor

S, SH — S as in especially → **CH, J** — J as in jar → **CH'** — CH as in church

Depicts the outline of the throat

NG — NG as in king → **H** — H as in home

Vowels:

Depiction of Heaven · Depiction of Earth — Depiction of Man |

Ŭ — OO as in too **I** — I as in inch

A — A as in father → **YA** — YA as in yacht

Ŏ — E as in term → **YŎ** — YOU as in young

O — O as in old → **YO** — YO as in yoke

U — U as in June → **YU** — YOU as in you

85

Chosŏn's Fight for Freedom

Historical Background

Until the late 18th century Koreans knew very little about the Western world. They thought that civilization had its source in China and India. However, during the reign of King Sŏnjo in the first part of the 17th century, Korean envoys returning from Peking brought home maps of Europe and books on Catholicism written by Matteo Ricci, an Italian missionary. And then in 1631 Jan Janse Weltevree, a Dutch navigator who had drifted to the southern islands of Korea, lived in Seoul in the employ of the king's army. Here he manufactured weapons, including cannons, and married a Korean woman. By this time European telescopes, clocks, and books were brought back from China by the Korean diplomatic missions.

In 1653, another drifting ship reached the southern shore of Chejudo Island. According to the records of the time 36 men of "astoundingly strange and hitherto totally unknown appearance and feature" landed. The Korean helpers noted that they had "blue eyes and yellow hair," and "strangely high noses and mustaches." These mariners were taken to the capital, Seoul, where they joined the army, and most of them lived on in Korea for the rest of their lives. But in 1666, eight of them returned to the Netherlands. One of them, Hendrik Hamel, wrote stories of his

Illustrations from Hendrik Hamel's book, Description du Royaume Coree, showing the Dutch ship which was shipwrecked off the coast of Chejudo Island and Hamel's crew coming ashore.

adventures in Korea, which were published in Amsterdam in 1668. Hamel's book was the first published in the West about Korea.

In 1777, during the regin of King Chŏngjo, the Catholic church was first introduced into Korea via China, and the king's court, finding it incompatible with Confucian teachings, prohibited its mission under severe penalty. Then in 1839 came the first persecutions of a large number of believers; three French missionaries and 30 Korean followers were executed.

After the massacre of the Catholics and the firing on foreign war vessels, the French and the United States governments held China responsible for those acts, assuming that she was the suzerain of Korea. But China declared Korea to be an independent nation. Seeing the influence of Japan

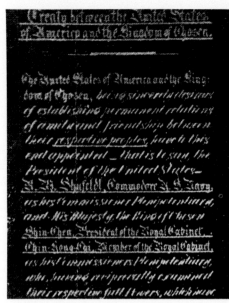

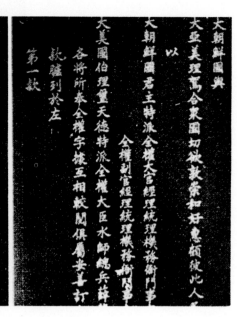

Lucius Foote, the first U.S. minister to Korea who served from 1883-85 (top) and Min Yong-ik, the first Korean envoy to the U.S. who served from 1883-84 (above). At upper right is a copy of the Treaty of Peace, Amity, Commerce and Navigation that was signed between the Chosŏn Kingdom and the U.S. in 1882.

spread over Korea, however, China was alarmed. In order to maintain the balance of foreign power in Korea, China urged the Korean court to conclude treaties with Western countries. As a result a treaty of amity and commerce was signed between Korea and the United States in 1882, and in the next two years England, Germany, Austria, Russia, Italy, and France followed suit, with the exchange of diplomatic missions. Korea had made her first debut on the international stage.

From the very beginning the Western nations, as well as Russia and Japan, encouraged the Korean government to heed no "foreign" interference. Specifically, they were anxious to get rid of the Chinese interests and influence in the Korean peninsula. Thus the British moved ships to a Korean port near the coast and kept them there until China withdrew its forces from Seoul, and the British agreed to permit the Japanese to dispatch troops to Korea "in case of emergency." This privilege gave the Japanese their opening opportunity in 1894. Then the Japanese government launched, with the approval of the British and American governments, a treacherous war against China.

The Japanese created the necessary "emergency" in Korea and sent more troops. As Japanese numbers increased steadily, the Chinese likewise increased their troops in Korea.

On July 16, 1894, the Anglo-Japanese Treaty was signed. A few days later the Japanese government's military forces seized the Korean royal palace and proclaimed the king's 80-year-old father as a regent, whom they could use to control the Korean government. The regent was forced to sign a "declaration of war" against China. Then the Japanese promptly launched attacks upon the Chinese forces. In a few months, it was clear that the well-prepared Japanese were decisively superior to the Chinese armies.

Soon there was a peace treaty between Japan and China. Japan gained China's acquiescence to have the sole maintenance of Japanese troops in Korea, with General Miura Goro as the Foreign Minister in Seoul. This was one of the most significant turning points in Korean history because once again Korea was slowly coming under the Japanese occupation.

King Kojong (r. 1863-1907),
the 26th monarch of
Chosŏn, and Queen Min.

U.S. Secretary of
War William H. Taft

Japanese Prime Minister
Taro Katsura

Queen Min of Korea, resenting the growing power of the Japanese, worked quietly to protect Korea's independence. The anti-Japanese group centered in or around Queen Min.

This was soon noticed by General Miura and he gave order to eliminate her. On October 8, 1885, the Japanese troops attacked the palace and overcame the queen's bodyguard. The queen fled, but Japanese troops pursued and hacked her to death with their swords. The next morning they burned the queen's body at the palace court. This was the most barbarous murder of any sovereign in modern times.

This incident prompted another Anglo-Japanese treaty concluded in February 1902. Great Britain specifically pledged to defend the "independence and territorial integrity" of Korea. Russia and France pledged themselves to the same principle. All powers were avowedly in agreement on a joint guarantee of "collective security" for Korea. Nevertheless, the Japanese encroachment in Korea grew in intensity along political as well as economic lines.

Now the only power challenging Japan in Korea was Russia. Japan determined to attempt the elimination of the Russians by military means. In 1903 Japan strengthened her alliance with Great Britain and the United States and started to make demands which were a prelude to the war with Russia the following year. Finally, with the arbitration of President Theodore Roosevelt of the United States, the two nations (Japan and Russia) laid down arms and signed the Portsmouth Treaty, which was supposed to restore peace in the Far East. Peace, however, was bought at the cost of Korea.

In this pact, President Roosevelt specifically approved "the establishment by Japanese troops of a suzerainty over Korea." And also the Japanese government declared that "Japan does not harbor any aggressive designs whatever on the Philippines."

With this treaty, the Japanese thus obtained influential support from the British and the Americans for their domination over Korea. Japan's victory over Russia in 1905 gave Japan exclusive power in Korea. On November 15, the Japanese demanded that all Korean foreign relations be placed in the hands of Japan. The Korean emperor refused. Japanese troops surrounded the palace in an attempt to force the emperor and his cabinet to accept the Japanese demands. The Japanese dispatched messengers to the custodian of the imperial seal, took the seal from him by force, and attached it to the new "treaty" which made Korea a Japanese protectorate. All the foreign embassies in Seoul watched these proceedings for two days without a single gesture of help. Extracted under direct and immediate duress, force and violence, and without the consent of the Korean sovereign, the "treaty" was nevertheless carried out. Surprisingly the American government was the first to approve the Japanese action and ordered the Seoul legation closed. The Korean emperor's special envoy had already reached Washington, but President Roosevelt refused to see him. A second special envoy followed, who on behalf of the Korean emperor, informed the American State Department on December 11 that the protocol of November 17 had not been agreed to by him, and that his seal had been affixed under duress. Secretary of State Elihu Root replied that he was unable to take any official cognizance of this envoy.

Although by this time the Japanese were not in full military control, the office of the Japanese Resident-General was established at Seoul, to replace the administrative power of the Korean government at the top level.

Emperor Kojong sent his personal emissary headed by Yi Chun to the Second Hague Peace Conference at The Hague in 1907. Bearing the emperor's message with him, Yi Chun placed Korea's cause before the world diplomats. He denounced the Japanese usurpation of Korea and called for world sympathy toward Korea's effort to restore her sovereignty. But the statesmen of the world failed to heed Korea's plea. Then Yi Chun, in a last desperate appeal for justice, cut his stomach with his pocket knife and died. Japan was furiously angered over this and threatened the lives of the emperor and his cabinet ministers. The Japanese hurriedly tightened their grip over Korean government officials and permitted no official to be appointed without their approval. Finally on August 22, 1910, Japan officially annexed Korea. Thus the curtain was closed on the Chosŏn Kingdom after a reign of 519 years and 27 kings.

During the following 35 years of Japanese occupation, Korea underwent extreme suppression and hardship. As their colonial policy made headway and the enslavement of the people was stepped up, the Japanese actively worked to exterminate the Korean heritage. They forced use of the Japanese language and prohibited use of the Korean language. During this period the Japanese also placed the 33 members of the Korean Language Society in jail. Five were eventually found innocent and released. Sixteen were condemned. The remaining 12 were moved from jail to jail for a year while their cases were pending at the prosecutor's office. The 16 condemned languished in jail for the duration of the Pacific War. Two died in their cells. History has little parallel to this punishment of scholars whose only crime was that they loved their own language. The study of Korean history was prohibited in the schools. The Japanese burned all the books written in Korean and even forced Koreans to adopt Japanese names. They finally forced Koreans to worship the Japanese Shinto god.

Early in 1919, after World War I ended, the opportunity came for the Korean people to reassert their right to freedom from tyranny. The Korean people were greatly stimulated by President Woodrow Wilson's doctrine of the Fourteen Points, including the "self-determination of peoples." He had proposed "a free, open-minded, and absolutely impartial adjustment of all colonial claims, based upon a strict observance of the principle that

Credentials of the envoys to the Second Hague Peace Conference bearing the seal of "Emperor" Kojong (below) and some clippings from European newspapers about the envoys protesting Japan's attempt to colonize Korea (bottom).

A modern depiction of the 33 leaders of the March 1, 1919 Independence Movement meeting to sign the Korean Declaration of Independence.

in determining all such questions of sovereignty the interests of the populations concerned must have equal weight with the equitable claims of the government whose title is to be determined." On March 1, 1919, while the Versailles peace talks were in session in Paris, Korea's old Emperor Kojong died mysteriously. A myriad of people began mourning his loss simultaneously. At noon on this day Koreans in Seoul gathered at Pagoda Park, where a Declaration of Independence was read aloud by 33 leading patriots representing the 20 million people who had signed the declaration. They shouted *"Taehan Tongnip Manse!"* (Long live Korean independence!), and with the prohibited national Korean flag in hand, they demonstrated peacefully. This spontaneous demonstration prompted by the king's death took place simultaneously over almost the entire country. The leading patriots sent a note to the Japanese government and presented a special appeal to the American president, Woodrow Wilson, and to the chairman of the Paris Peace Conference.

In a short time, the Korean independence movement spread all over the world in a concerted action between patriots at home and abroad. To suppress the movement, the Japanese government ordered out police and army units, which wounded many peaceful demonstrators and massacred a large number. Those who escaped were pressed into jails, flogged, and tortured.

C.W. Kendall, who witnessed the entire independence movement, described in his book, *The Truth About Korea*, "In the first three months over 50,000 Koreans have been killed or wounded. The horror and brutality of some of the deeds committed are beyond belief."

The independence movement contributed to the development of a spirit of national unity among people of all classes and ages. And it brought Korea's plight to world attention for the first time. It also taught the Japanese government that they could not rule Korea by mere force alone. Korean history will never show a more glorious page than the record of March 1, 1919, nor portray more heroic actions than those of the men, women and even children who dared to hold aloft their

Women demonstrating for Korean independence from Japan on March 1, 1919, some members of the Korean Righteous Army which fought a guerrilla-style war against the Japanese, and some members of the Korean Revolution Army in the U.S. (from top to bottom).

national flag and sound the immortal cry of *"Taehan Tongnip Manse!"*

Inside Korea, several secret organizations were formed which maintained nationwide contact, but the independence movement was far more active abroad. Many organized groups carried on the movement in China, Manchuria, Hawaii, and in America.

In the summer of 1941, in the Atlantic Charter, President Franklin D. Roosevelt of the U.S. and Prime Minister Winston Churchill of Great Britain declared that "they respect the right of all peoples to choose the form of government under which they will live, and they wish to see sovereign rights and self-government restored to those who have been forcibly deprived of them." At this juncture Japan was invading China in an extension of her conquest of Manchuria. On the eve of World War II, she threw her lot in with Nazi Germany and Fascist Italy by signing the Axis Pact. On December 7, 1941 Japan began a war against America and England in the Pacific theater by attacking Pearl Harbor.

As the war continued, Japan ran short of manpower and Korea was forced to supply the need. The Japanese governor-general redoubled efforts to draft Korean youth under the so-called "volunteer" system. The Japanese government also forced Koreans to work in mines, factories and military construction abroad. As the strain on Japanese resources reached the breaking point and defeat loomed over her, the actions of her government in Korea became more and more desperate and cruel. All the rice production went to Japan as well as all the cattle. Any metal objects including scrap iron, brass pots and dishes, even metal spoons and chopsticks were seized for the munitions factories. But with the surrender of Japan to the Allies on August 15, 1945, Korea at last had a viable hope for its own independent government.

A modern depiction of educator Yi Sŭng-hun lecturing students on the virtues of self-reliance and independence.

Cultural Background

In 1631 during the reign of King Injo of the Chosŏn Kingdom, the teachings of the West, such as Lessin's theology, Cicero's philosophy and Euclid's geometry, were introduced to the educated class of Korea by Jesuit missionaries living in China. In 1631, new products of Western civilization such as telescopes, clocks, maps, new muskets, astronomical instruments, books on Occidental customs and manners, and paintings in Western style were brought to Korea.

These new products and ideas of Western civilization brought about significant changes among the Korean people and their way of thinking. The calendar system was westernized and the modernization movement was started in everything from agriculture to sanitation. Christianity, which had begun to come to Korea in the middle of the 17th century, established a firm foothold in Korea during the 19th century. Korean emissaries were sent to Peking to invite Christian preachers to Korea and also to bring in religious publications. A request was made to the Pope in Rome for permission to establish parishes in Korea.

The significant changes that were coming within Korea and in her relations with an expanding world in the latter half of the 19th century culminated in the rise of a native religious movement drawing its inspiration from both historical Korean experience and the currents of modern

reforms. This new religion was called Tonghak which means "Eastern Learning." In a sense it was a reaction against Catholicism, which was known as "Western Learning" in Korea. It was also inspired by the political and social inequality caused by the discrimination between the ruling aristocratic class and the commoners, since the masses suffered severe hardships under the corrupt rulers. In these respects it was a reform movement as well as an anti-foreign expression.

The founder of the Tonghak school of religion, Ch'oe Che-u (pen name-Suun), readily admitted the syncretic nature of his theology, typical of Korean religion through out the ages. "Our way is originally not Buddhism, Confucianism, or Taoism," he wrote. His teaching asserted that through self-discipline and cultivation one can obtain the divine virtue of being able to influence everything without conscious effort or volition. He claimed further that man could not be saved simply by passive acceptance of God, but that only through his own efforts could man cultivate God's good graces and finally become identified with him.

In order to discover a new way for the salvation of the nation and well-being for the people, Ch'oe wandered about the whole country for 21 years. His zeal and sincerity were so great that apparently Heaven was moved and at last, he found his answer and went forth to preach. He said, "I have found the new, true way. Many a man suffered death because the old way was wrong. From now on we must live a new life in accordance with the new way. The old way was discriminative; a few enjoyed wealth and power while the majority were doomed to suffering and oppression. From now on we will live a life of serving the people as we do Heaven. We will live a happy life because we will live the life of liberty and equality."

His doctrine was based on the theory of *chigi* which means "ultimate force or pure force." The ultimate force is the pure force differentiated into a myriad of concrete things. In the light of modern science, the life of an individual seems understandable and yet of life there is far more to be grasped. Here the ultimate force is Heaven's truth or God. According to Ch'oe's teaching only through his own self-discipline could man find or understand the pure force and finally become identified with God. Therefore this theory may be explained in three steps. First, the ultimate or pure force, or God, is represented in each individual life. Second, of all individual lives, human life is manifested as God's image; thus men are all equal in their rights. Third, when one cultivates oneself and attains a perfect standard he is the same God. On the contrary when a man commits evil or sins, he will be degraded to the status of an animal. In other words, character has different degrees. The standard of morality in Tonghak is that the end of a man's conduct is not only of benefit to the individual but to the whole society, nation, and the world.

There is no doubt that the Tonghak religion was influenced by the other traditional religions. The founder, Ch'oe, aimed at a religious system, in his own words, "fusing into one the ethics of Confucianism, the Taoist cultivation of energy, and the cultivative character and rebirth in Buddhism." Furthermore, he even introduced the idea of the personal God of Catholicism.

In reality, Tonghak brought very important new ideas to Koreans. For example the idea of dignity and equality of all men led to a new democratic society. The idea of the new nationalism eventually influenced the independence movement of March 1, 1919. Later the Tonghak name was changed to Ch'ŏndogyo (Religion of the Heavenly Way).

A contemporary painting of Chŏn Pong-chun leading Tonghak rebels during the 1894 Tonghak Revolt.

The Republic of Korea (1948-   )

As a result of the Japanese surrender to World War II Allies on August 15, 1945, Korea was liberated from 36 years of Japanese domination. However, the liberation was based on earlier international politics, the first agreement having been made at the Cairo Conference in a joint declaration by President Franklin D. Roosevelt, Prime Minister Winston Churchill, and Generalissimo Chiang Kai-Shek on December 1, 1943, which stated, "the aforesaid three great powers, mindful of the enslavement of the people of Korea, are determined that in due course Korea shall become free and independent." These three powers reaffirmed their Cairo pledge in the Potsdam Declaration of July 26, 1945, which was later endorsed by the Soviet Union when it declared war against Japan on August 9, 1945. Thus, before the surrender of Japan, four principal powers publicly supported the course of Korean independence.

Meantime, the United States made overtures to the Soviet Union. President Harry S. Truman sent a special mission to Moscow to sound out Stalin's intentions. The American historian Herbert Feis writes in his book, *Between War and Peace:*

> The mention of Korea was brief. Hopkins said the American government thought it would be desirable that the four most interested powers share in the trusteeship over Korea, the Soviet Union, the United States, China, and Great Britain. Its duration might be left open. It would certainly run for five or ten years, perhaps as long as 25. Stalin said he fully agreed.

Therefore the plans for Korean independence could be implemented only by military occupation, and two separate zones of occupation became

Residents of Seoul rejoicing at the news of Japan's surrender to the U.S. and Korea's liberation on August 15, 1945.

Stalin, Roosevelt and Churchill at the Yalta Conference in February 1945.

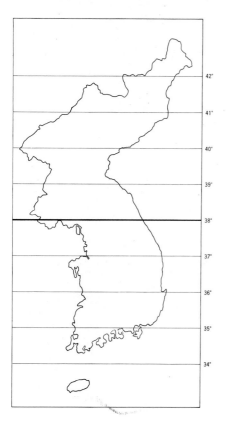

a fact with the entry of Russian combat troops into North Korea on August 10, 1945, and entry of the American occupation troops into South Korea on September 8, 1945. The military leaders of the United States and the Soviet Union had agreed that the Soviet troops would accept the Japanese surrender north of the 38th parallel and that American troops would accept the surrender south of it. Thus the arbitrary and crucial division of Korea came about.

Korea's division does not compare with the division of other countries. The German division came as a penalty for the war the Germans lost. The Chinese partition resulted from an unfinished revolution of their own. The Vietnamese sectioning was the legacy of an incomplete anti-colonial war. All these cases in their own different ways have sufficient reasons for national division. By contrast, Korea's was the sheer outcome of power politics between the United States and the Soviet Union. It was indeed a bitter pill to swallow for the Koreans. The national independence for which they had fought for 35 years was only to be had at the price of the country's dismemberment. Subsequently, the problem of Korean unification and independence was turned over to the United States and the Soviet Union. A preliminary conference between the two occupying authorities was held in early 1946, but the conference was unsuccessful.

On November 15, 1947, the United Nations established a United Nations Temporary Commission on Korea to expedite independence. Underlying the United Nations resolution was an emphasis upon the formation of a national government for a united Korea. The United Nations Temporary Commission on Korea held its first meeting in Seoul in January 1948. The Commission sent official communications to the military commanders in North and South Korea. The American commander in South Korea replied to the communication immediately, but the Russian commander in North Korea refused even to accept it. Subsequent attempts by the Commission to visit North Korea were blocked by the Communists.

Following the failure of the Commission to gain entry into North Korea or even to establish any contact with the Soviet authorities, the Commission consulted with the Interim Committee of the United Nations General Assembly. The predominant opinion among the delegates of the Interim Committee was that the recommendations of the General Assembly were

A ceremony at the capitol celebrating the founding of the Republic of Korea on August 15, 1948.

clear, and the existing conditions made it impossible to hold elections for a national government in both North and South Korea. The conclusions of the Interim Committee were embodied in a resolution adopted on February 26, 1948.

Therefore, by a resolution of the United Nations, elections under United Nations supervision were held in South Korea only on May 10, 1948. This resulted in the formation of a Korean National Assembly and in the establishing of the government of the Republic of Korea with Syngman Rhee (Yi Sŭng-man) as the first president. The new republic was officially inaugurated on August 15, 1948, the third anniversary of the liberation of Korea from Japanese rule, and governmental authority was promptly transferred from the American military government to the new republic. Ten days later, North Korea established the Democratic People's Republic of Korea with Kim Il-sung as the first president.

At the third session of the United Nations General Assembly in Paris in December 1948, the United Nations Temporary Commission on Korea took the stand that the Republic of Korea was the legitimate government of all Korea and recommended recognition by the United Nations. The General Assembly thereupon adopted a resolution recognizing the Republic of Korea as the only legitimate government of all Korea. It appointed another commission to continue the work of the Temporary Commission, to supervise the withdrawal of the occupation forces, and to use its offices to bring about the unification of Korea.

At dawn on June 25, 1950, the North Korean Communist forces launched an armed aggression against the Republic of Korea, across the 38th parallel. On the same day the United Nations Security Council met and adopted a resolution finding that the attack by North Korean forces constituted a breach of the peace, and calling for the immediate cessation of hostilities and the withdrawal of the North Korean forces to the 38th parallel. On June 27 the Security Council met again. The United Nations Commission on Korea reported that the situation in the peninsula showed possibilities of rapid deterioration. Seoul fell to the Communists on June 28, and the Communist forces surged down to the south.

The Security Council therefore adopted a resolution which stated that

A map of the initial invasion routes used by the North Koreans when they launched the Korean War (below). North Korean tanks spearheading the invasion of Seoul, June 28, 1950 (lower right). Millions of North Koreans fled southward over destroyed bridges ahead of hordes of Chinese troops who entered the war in October 1950 (bottom right).

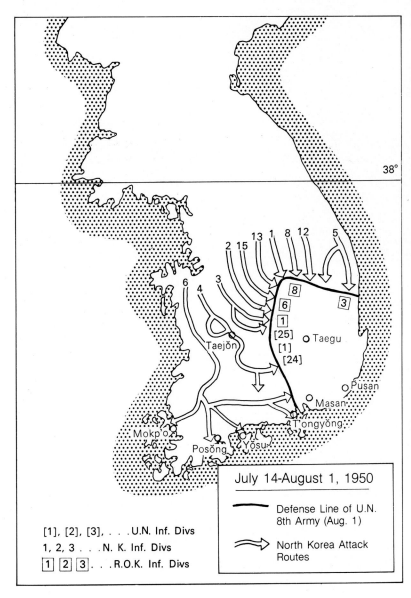

July 14-August 1, 1950

⎯⎯⎯ Defense Line of U.N. 8th Army (Aug. 1)

⟹ North Korea Attack Routes

[1], [2], [3], . . .U.N. Inf. Divs

1, 2, 3 . . .N. K. Inf. Divs

[1] [2] [3]. . .R.O.C. Inf. Divs

the authorities of North Korea had not complied with the resolution of June 25, and that urgent military measures were required to restore international peace and security. It recommended that the members of the United Nations furnish such assistance to the Republic of Korea as might be necessary to repel the armed attack and to restore international peace and security in the area. Eventually, 16 nations contributed military units and over 40 provided material aid.

The first United Nations ground troops were thrown into battle on July 4, 1950 but the defense on the Kŭmgang River faltered and the battle of Taejŏn was lost to the Communists. Then United Nations forces pulled back to the Naktonggang River. General Douglas MacArthur personally commanded the Inch'ŏn Landing which brought a sound defeat to the North Korean forces. General MacArthur recaptured Seoul on September 28, 1950, and the victorious United Nations forces pursued the retreating enemy across the 38th parallel. P'yŏngyang, the North

Korean capital, fell to the advancing United Nations forces on October 9 and the United Nations forces reached the Manchurian border on October 26.

But on November 26, the Chinese Communists crossed the Yalu River in human-wave tactics, trapping the United Nations forces and obliging them to bear a general retreat. The Chinese Communists crossed the 38th parallel on December 25, and entered Seoul again on January 4, 1951. But the enemy's offensives were stopped by the command of General Matthew M. Ridgeway, striking back with superior firepower. Seoul was recaptured by the United Nations forces for the second time on March 18, 1951. The United Nations units began an offensive again in late May that pushed the Communists back beyond the 38th parallel

On June 23, 1951, Russia's United Nations delegate Jacob Malik made a proposal that truce talks be opened. The Korean War had reached a stalemate, ending with a negotiated truce signed on July 27, 1953. The fighting stopped at ten o'clock that night along a 193-kilometer front across the peninsula.

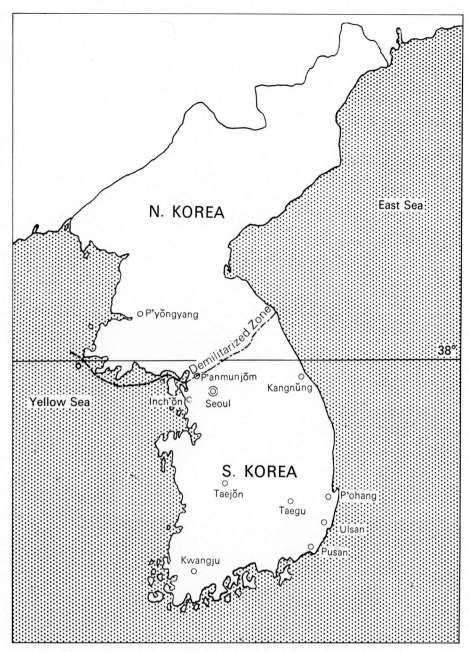

The map shows the Korean peninsula with the following labels:

N. KOREA — P'yŏngyang — East Sea — Demilitarized Zone — 38° — P'anmunjŏm — Kangnŭng — Yellow Sea — Inch'ŏn — Seoul — S. KOREA — Taejŏn — Taegu — P'ohang — Ulsan — Pusan — Kwangju

A U.N. Security Council Meeting in June 1950 (top left). General Douglas MacArthur inspecting U.N. forces on the front lines following the Inch'ŏn Landing (left and center). Two men draw a line on a map of Korea to mark a 193-kilometer front along which fighting stopped at 10 p.m. July 27, 1953 (upper right).

The Republic of Korea forces suffered nearly 300,000 casualties and United Nations forces another 30,000. South Korea alone lost hundreds of thousands of civilians, and more than 100,000 children were orphaned. But these figures cannot convey the horrors which the war inflicted on the men and women of Korea for three years.

A divided Korea is an economic and political anomaly which cannot happily survive. The Korean people are one people, historically, ethnically and culturally. The present two halves of the divided nation complement each other and Koreans of both halves would like to share a unified government. The division of Korea stands in the way of a truly permanent peace in the Far East. Almost all Koreans understand these basic facts, and whatever their other differences, all are united in the firm conviction that Korea should be unified. In an era of negotiation and political elasticity, the United States and the Soviet Union ought to be working toward overdue talks on Korean unification. However, history has taught the Koreans that it must be largely up to their own people, of both North and South, to achieve the goal of uniting their fatherland.

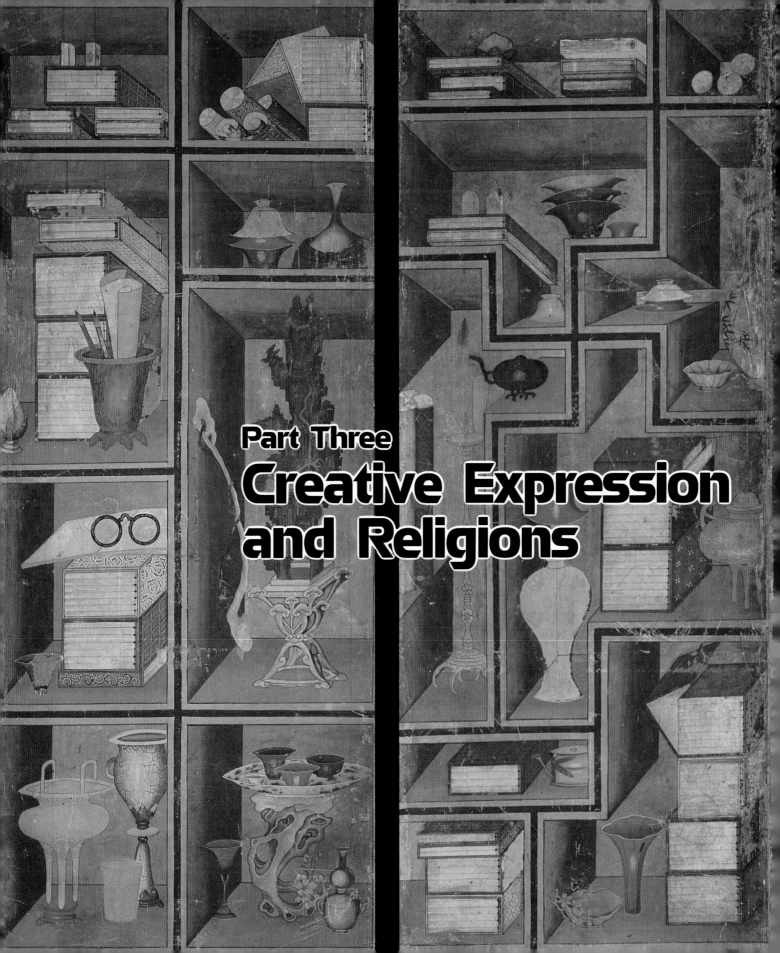

Part Three
Creative Expression and Religions

Arts

Korea was known in the past for its beautiful scenery and delightful climate. In the 20th century it has assumed a new role. Important and romantic archaeological discoveries have been made in the past few decades. The land is full of historic ruins of gardens, temples, and pagodas, of memorial tablets and masonry walls and long forgotten palaces. Stone Buddhas carved more than 2,000 years ago stand in mountain caves or emerge from great boulders on hillsides. But, above all, there are the graves, and in some parts of the country huge mounds, numbering many hundreds, which rise above the remains of rulers and the nobility of an ancient state, hiding a history that until the relatively recent past has been little more than hearsay.

Because the Korean peninsula is isolated from the continent of China, Koreans developed their own cultural pattern from the very beginning. The characteristics of their ancient art can be seen distinctly at the time when the three kingdoms started developing in their own ways after their founding.

The Koguryŏ people expressed their own adventurous spirit in their fine arts. They occupied a wide area extending north and south of the Yalu River, and the old tombs which lie scattered along the banks of the Yalu are on a grand scale. There are tombs with murals of the "Four Gods," "Korean Wrestling," the "Dance by Three Women," the "Hunting Scene," the "Dragon God," and the "War Horse."

The ceilings of these tombs are also lavishly decorated with figures of lotus petals, fancy animals, and cocks, together with symbols of the sun and of the moon. These examples show the masculinity of the powerful Koguryŏ people. Particularly, refined grace and style are shown in the painting of the "Four Gods." A small part of the Koguryŏ architecture also can be seen in the structure of the old tombs.

Wall paintings from several ancient tombs.

102

Two tombs have so far been excavated near Kongju and Puyŏ in the old Paekche domain. The Paekche people made an effort to carve Buddhist statues, erect stone pagodas, and build Buddhist temples after the introduction of Buddhism. Paekche's murals reflect softer and less masculine features than those of Koguryŏ. Paekche's development of a higher level of art can be seen in the few decorated rooftiles and floortiles preserved in the National Museum.

Shilla began to form their art with the introduction of Buddhism. The world-famous Ch'ŏmsŏngdae (astronomical observatory) was erected in 647. The observatory represents the Oriental idea of astronomy mathematically, in its structural scale and proportion. The Shilla images of Buddha introduced fresh and graceful lines, surpassing the style of the Chinese during the era. The bronze images of seated Maitreya or the statues of the thinking Buddha are good examples. Among the most famous

Gold crown ornaments (below) excavated from the tomb of Paekche's King Muryŏng-wang (r. 501-523). A gilt-bronze Maitreya Buddha of the Three Kingdoms era, late 6th century (right).

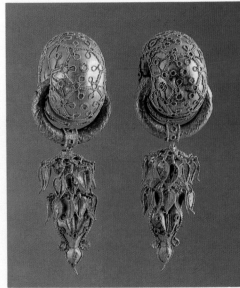

artworks of old Shilla is a golden crown excavated from one of the old tombs in Kyŏngju. It is in the form of three tall conventionalized trees rising from a bank of gold, which encircle an openwork peaked cap terminating in two winglike flaps of intricate lacy design. Small, round, gold spangles are attached at numerous places over the surface of the crown by means of fine twisted gold wires, and jade and glass comma-shaped beads, known as *magatama*, or "crooked beads," are similarly fastened here and there on the crown and at the ends of long "drops" falling over the ears. Altogether, their filgree and granule technique are strikingly unique in Asia.

As Shilla became a peninsula-wide society, artists integrated the delicate beauty of Paekche and the grandiosity of Koguryŏ to create a new brilliance in their art. The Shilla style became one of wholesome beauty as it expanded north and south during the unification. Shilla's love of nature

Gold crown with pendants, Shilla, 5th-6th century, excavated from the Heavenly Horse Tomb in Kyŏngju (left) and gold ear pendants, Shilla, 5th-6th century, excavated from another tomb in Kyŏngju (above).

Sarira containers of Shilla origin decorated with a variety of Buddhist motifs.

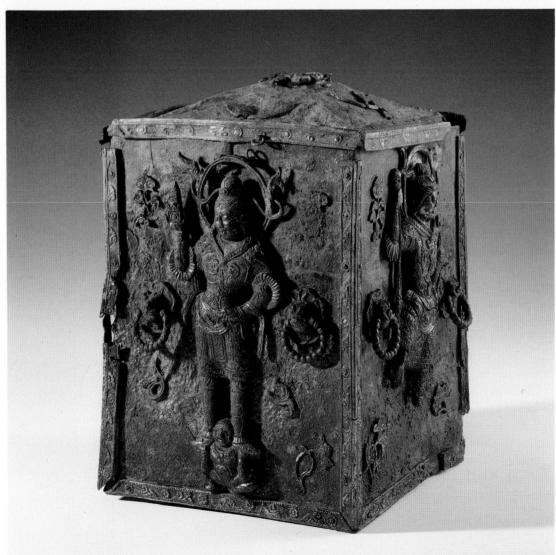

and orderliness is evident in the architectural techniques employed in such works as Anapchi, a manmade lake; P'osŏkchŏng, an abalone-shaped stone channel through which wine cups were floated; Pulguksa, the "Temple of the Buddha Land;" and Sŏkkuram, a secluded temple in a stone cave. This stone cave temple is a manifestation of their more refined, almost perfect sense of beauty. The almost 3.1-meter-tall principal image is Sakyamuni, the Historic Buddha, sitting crossed-legged with his robe draped over his left shoulder. The wheel sign, a preaching symbol, was placed in the center of the cave so as to be admired by the many various images which are carved on the wall around it. These granite sculptures, in which the Shilla people's skillful modeling treatments and their refined techniques in achieving life-like appearances are displayed, reflect clearly the Shilla Kingdom's national traits and local characteristics. The famous bell of the Pongdŏksa Temple was cast about the same time and displays the creative power of the Shilla people in the expression of its beauty.

The kingdom of Koryŏ established the Tohwawon, an office of painting, in order to promote this art and to safeguard its creative activities. The governmental bureau of painting was to inherit and to transmit the classics of ancient painting. Naturally the quantity and quality of paintings were greatly enhanced as a by-product of this governmental policy. The art of

Anapchi, a recently restored pond in Kyŏngju that was part of a detached palace.

108

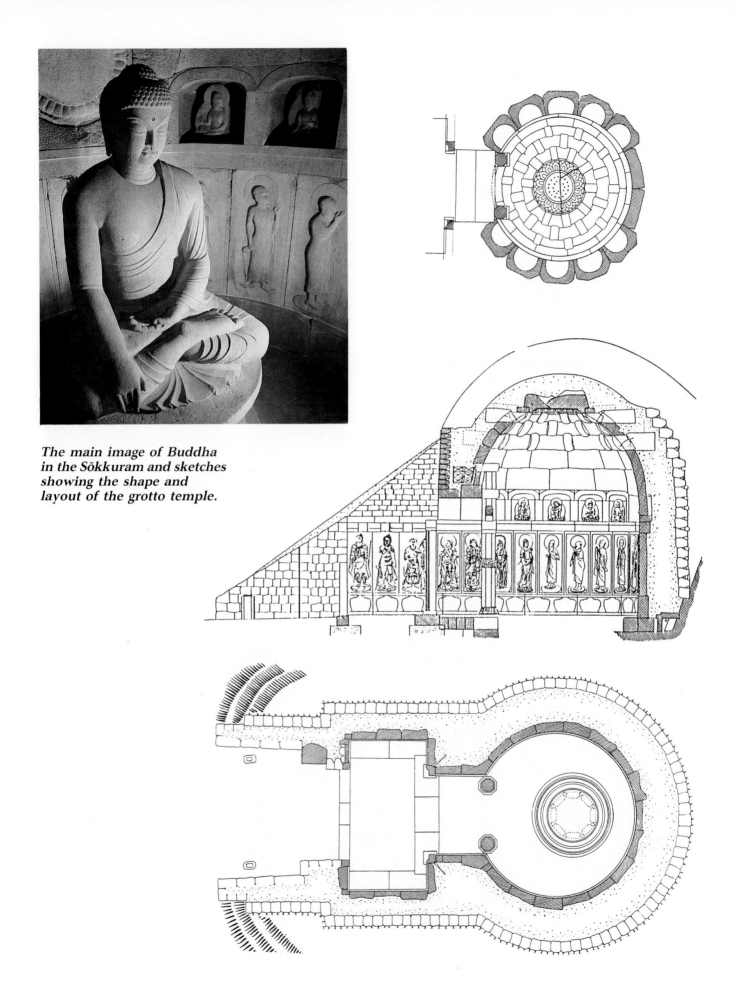

The main image of Buddha in the Sŏkkuram and sketches showing the shape and layout of the grotto temple.

Koryŏ in general fell behind that of Shilla due to the conditions that Koryŏ had to face. Despite a general decline of industrial arts, the production of Ch'ŏngja (celadon) is one of the best representations of the Koryŏ people. Its color, form, and decoration are the special contributions of the Koryŏ people to ceramic art. Their inlaying technique, particularly, was a new method in ceramics. Lightness and exquisite differentiation of color in the porcelain, such as pure white, grey white and blue, became the essence of the Korean technique.

The ceramic art of the Chosŏn Kingdom may be studied in three categories: that following the tradition of Koryŏ celadon, white porcelain after the fashion of Koryŏ white porcelain, and blue-and-white porcelain influenced by the Chinese. Compared with the aristocratic pottery of the Koryŏ Kingdom, that of Chosŏn lost much of its delicacy and decorative design, which were replaced by simplicity and naivety. The simplicity of form and lack of decoration are a direct expression of the utilitarian nature of the ware and of the character of the common people. Because of an abundance of natural resources for ceramics, Korean pottery enjoyed prosperity until the end of the 16th century. Plain white porcelain, much influenced by Koryŏ porcelain, achieved a sense of originality in its shapes. White porcelain items with underglaze, and copper, blue, iron, and famous powder-green decorations were also produced in limited numbers. The quiet hue of celadon, the monotonous tone of the Chosŏn white porcelain, and the simple colors of white clothing reflect the Korean people's traditional love for plainness and sincerity. When one looks at Chosŏn white porcelain, he is charmed by the variations of subtle white color and the simple shapes. There is a sense of immediacy and familiarity.

Some good examples of architecture of this period are Tongdaemun, the Great East Gate; Namdaemun, the Great South Gate; and the Secret Garden, all located in Seoul. The Secret Garden was constructed in such excellent harmony with its surroundings as to represent the best of the Korean technique of gardening, with its arrangements of belvederes, terraces, pavilions, and kiosks.

A celadon glazed porcelain jar with an inlaid decoration, Koryŏ, mid-12th century (left).

Celadon bottle, painted in underglaze iron, Koryŏ period, first half of 12th century (right).
Wine bottle, celadon glaze; painted in underglaze iron, Koryŏ period, 13th century (far right).

110

White porcelain jar with underglaze iron decoration, Chosŏn, 16th century.

White porcelain jar with underglaze cobalt blue decoration, Chosŏn, 16th century.

Namdaemun, Seoul's South Gate, was built in 1396 and reconstructed in 1448 (above). Puyongjŏng, a pavilion in Ch'angdŏkkung Palace (right). The throne in Kŭnjŏngjŏn, the main throne hall of Kyŏngbokkung Palace (far right).

Calligraphy

Korean calligraphy is the art of brush writing. Calligraphy, by long and exacting tradition, is considered a major art, equal to painting. Especially in Oriental art calligraphy and painting have been worked very closely from ancient times. Furthermore, the Korean artist had extensive association with poem-composing in addition to writing and drawing. Calligraphy in Korea has exerted a strong influence on social and cultural life. Especially in recent years, it has been widely recognized as an art stimulating modern abstract painting.

Historically, calligraphy flourished mostly during the Chosŏn Kingdom when Confucianism became the philosophy of the state and Confucian learning became the driving force in the development of its calligraphy arts. The history of Korean calligraphy is as old as the introduction of Chinese characters themselves, even though the exact date is as yet uncertain. The oldest inscription of calligraphy on a tombstone is on that of King Kwanggaet'o in T'ung-kou, Koguryŏ's capital city in South Manchuria, which was built in the fifth century. The antique and simple style of the inscription is a good illustration of ancient Koguryŏ calligraphy.

Paekche, another of the three kingdoms, left to posterity one of the most significant inscriptions in the history of Oriental calligraphy. The inscription carved on the Sat'aekchijŏkpi monument in the National Puyŏ museum is written in a unique style and with its solemnity, correct-

The 627-centimeter-high stele to King Kwanggaet'o in southern Manchuria and a detail of the inscription it bears. At the lower right is a detail of an epitaph on the reverse side of a land deed for the gravesite of Paekche's King Muryŏng that was excavated from his tomb.

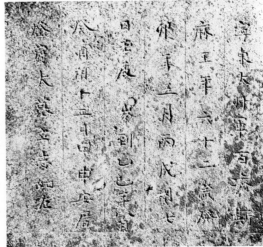

ness, and elegance, it is one of the best examples of Oriental calligraphy anywhere.

One of the most popular calligraphers of the Chosŏn Kingdom was Kim Ku (1488-1534). He studied the styles of such great Chinese calligraphers as Wang Hsi-Chih and further adopted aspects of each as his own style, which is still famous for its forceful strokes. Yang Sa-ŏn (1517-84) is one of the more important calligraphers in the history of the Chosŏn Kingdom. His works reached the highest level among all Korean calligraphy. In the writing of large characters he was second to none. There is one legendary story about his beautiful execution of large characters. On a piece of paper he wrote a character meaning "to fly" and put it on the wall of a room. One day that piece of paper suddenly began to float around the room for no apparent reason, and then disappeared altogether. It was later learned that Yang had died on that very day.

The calligraphy of the 19th century had to confront the problem of how to survive as an equal in rank with the other modern arts. It has not been so vital as the others, but its decline lies partly in the contemporary realities of society, pivoted on the criteria of the West. However, in the 20th century up until today there has been an ever increasing tendency, demonstrated even among Western painters, to search for the dynamic source of their own Occidental art through the study of the exquisiteness of Oriental painting and its artistic cousin, calligraphy.

Immortal and Crane *by Kim Hong-do (1745- after 1814), Chosŏn, ink and light colors on paper.*

117

**Viewing the Waterfall,
by Yi In-sang (died
1760 A.D.)**

**Orchids by
Kim Chŏng-hŭi
(1786-1857),Chosŏn,
hanging scroll, ink on paper.**

**Swimming Ducks by Hong
Se-sŏp (1831-?), Chosŏn,
hanging scroll, ink on paper.**

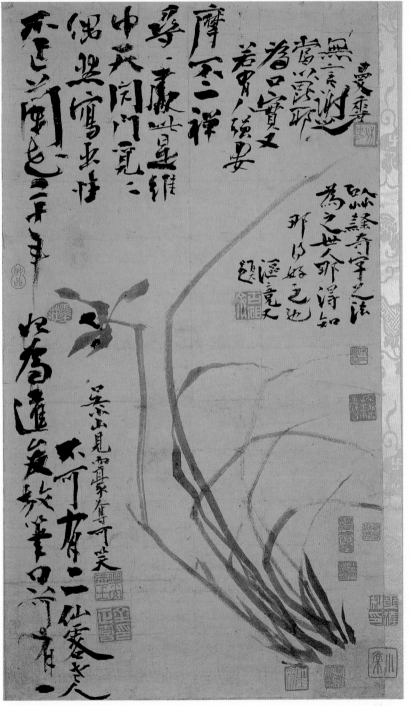

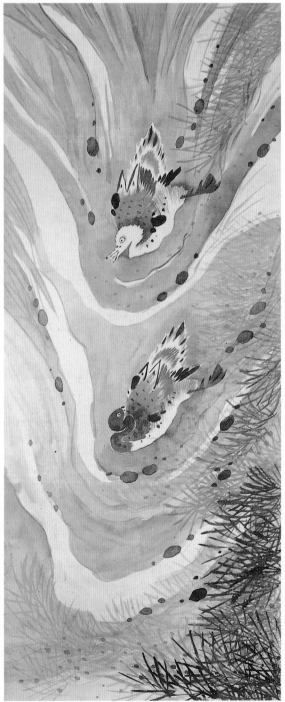

118

Except for some ancient tomb murals, few examples of paintings remain from the periods prior to Chosŏn. Paintings of the Chosŏn period show a harmonizing of Chinese influences with Korea's own native genius. Some of Chosŏn's most famous painters are represented here.

Ch'ongp'ung Valley *by Chŏng Sŏn (1676-1759), Chosŏn, dated 1739, hanging scroll, ink and light colors on silk.*

Tiger, artist unknown, hanging, scroll, ink and light colors on silk.

Landscape, *attributed to Yi Kyŏng-yun (1545-?), Chosŏn, hanging scroll, ink and light colors*
on silk.

Clear Skies over Mt. Inwang *by Chŏng Sŏn (1676-1759), Chosŏn,*
dated 1751, hanging scroll, ink and light colors on paper.

Women on Tano Day *by Shin Yun-bok (1758-?),*
Chosŏn, ink and color on paper.

Music and Dance

The first record of religious music in ancient Chosŏn is found to be associated with religious rites. People of Chosŏn expressed their prayers and thanksgiving by means of music. There were ceremonies for the worship of Heaven in the 10th and 12th lunar months, when people gathered together in all parts of the country and drank, sang, and danced for days. They were accompanied by simple musical instruments when they offered worship to Heaven for rain. Every year they gave performances to ask for blessings upon the sky, the earth, the forest, and the rivers. In the temples, musical instruments resounded with power and harmony so the ancestral spirits would hear the music. Worshipers chanted religious hymns to all that were present and to the whole manifestation of nature and art.

The people of Koguryŏ, who had had more frequent contacts with the northern part of China, adopted the Central Asian musical instruments. Her citizenry assimilated and created a national music collection which had more than 30 instruments. But most significant of all, they invented their own musical instrument, the *kŏmun-go*, or the "black harp," in the

A kŏmun-go.

7th century. This long, six-stringed zither has strings stretched over 16 movable bridges and is tuned with round pegs which hold the strings at one end of the instrument. It is played with a plectrum held in the right hand, while the left stops the strings at the various frets and produces the characteristic long, wavering vibrato and microtonal slide.

The Shilla Kingdom is responsible for the development of the *kayagŭm* zither. This 12-stringed zither, like the *kŏmun-go*, can be used in ceremonial ensemble music, as a solo instrument, or as accompaniment for singing. However, unlike the *kŏmun-go*, the strings of the *kayagŭm* are plucked with the fleshy part of the finger, or else flicked with the finger snapped from behind the thumb, producing an entirely different tone quality. The *kayagŭm* is a purely native invention and it has remained the most important of all Korean musical instruments up to the present day.

A classical musician playing a taegŭm, *a transverse bamboo flute.*

123

A classical orchestra.

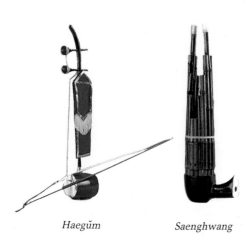

Haegŭm   Saenghwang

Changgo

During the reign of King Shinmun-wang (r. 839) there was a mountain in the Eastern Sea shaped like the head of a tortoise. On the mountain was a bamboo tree which, according to legend, parted into two in daytime and joined together at night. The king ordered this tree cut down and from it he made a flute called *taegŭm*, or large transverse flute, about 76 centimeters long. This flute has six finger holes and one larger hole covered by a membrane which vibrates when the instrument is blown, producing a rather piercing, pungent sound. Since its pitch is fixed, the rest of the orchestra tunes to it. It is used in native Korean music as accompaniment for songs and dances or as a solo instrument. At almost the same time the Shilla people also used the *pip'a* or lute. The lute comes in two versions; the Chinese version has four strings and the Korean one has five strings. Both are played with a plectrum or a straight stick.

Music of the Koryŏ Kingdom is usually divided into two areas. The first one is called *a-ak* or court music. Koryŏ's court music was influenced by Confucian ceremonial music. Court music included ritual ceremonies before the altars of heavenly gods at royal household shrines. For *a-ak* musicians used metal slab chimes, vertical and horizontal flutes, cylindrical oboes, *pip'a*, bowed long zithers, hourglass-shaped drums or *changgo*, and round drums.

Another area of Koryŏ music is *hyang-ak* or native music. This native or popular music was enriched with many new songs in the Koryŏ Kingdom. Musicians used a large variety of instruments such as the *kŏmun-go, kayagŭm, taegŭm, pip'a*, cylindrical oboe, flute, hourglass-shaped drum, and round drum.

One of the single most popular Korean musical instruments is the

124

changgo, an hourglass-shaped drum used first by the Koryŏ people. This
instrument is used for orchestra and ensemble music, chamber music,
and accompaniment for vocal and instrumental solos, and is also carried
by dancers. The drum has two heads, with the body tapering to a slender
waist between. The skin of the left end is thick and is struck with the
palm and that of the right end is thin and is struck with a stick. Thus
there are two contrasting timbres. The sound of the right end can be
adjusted by tightening or loosening the cords that stretch between the
two drum heads, holding them in place, although the instrument does
not have a definite pitch, like the Western timpani.

Another musical instrument the Koryŏ people developed was the
tanso or vertical flute. This is a small notched pipe with six finger holes,
including one on the underside of the instrument. It is played vertically
rather than transversely, as in the case of the taegŭm. It is of Korean
origin, although, of course, every nation at an early stage has produced
this sort of simple pipe. It is now employed exclusively in Korean music,
especially chamber music for duet or trio.

Piri or the oboe is also used for solo and chamber music. These cylindrical bamboo pipes have eight finger holes, including one on the underside, and employ a double reed, making them true oboes, or members
of the aulos family. There are both a Chinese and a Korean version,
showing some differences in the arrangement of the finger holes, the
Chinese version producing a heptatonic or seven-note scale, and the Korean
a pentatonic or five-note scale.

Another important instrument for court music is called p'yŏnjong or
bronze bells. Sixteen bells are hung in two rows on a wooden stand and

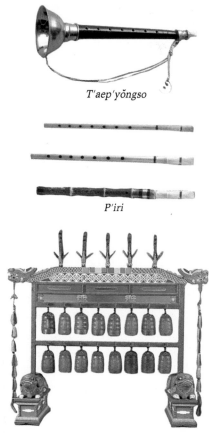

T'aep'yŏngso

P'iri

P'yŏnjong

are played by being struck with a hammer made of horn. The bells are all the same size, the pitch difference being effected by the varying thickness of the metal. They are always used in ceremonial, ritual music, as well as in Confucian rites, and also in court celebrations and ceremonies.

During the Chosŏn Kingdom music made great advances in original compositions, new arrangements of old ones, the remaking of old instruments, and the compiling of a guide to music. King Sejong, who invented the Korean alphabet, modernized the Korean musical theory and instruments with the help of Pak Yŏn. They published many music books and for the first time used a music scale. Pak Yŏn, who was a composer, a conductor, and an instrument maker, is considered the single most outstanding musician Korea has ever produced. He was also the organizer of the Imperial Music Department in his day and the founder of the Prince Yi Conservatory. Pak Yŏn was also responsible for providing the ritual music

for Korean Buddhism.

Recently a tendency has been growing among music lovers to give traditional music its rightful place in the life of the people. In this respect the National Classical Music Institute, formerly the Prince Yi Conservatory, has been busy training Korean musicians in the tasks of annotating, collecting and preserving a library and museum of Korea's traditional musical heritage. The museum now houses over 60 different kinds of traditional instruments.

Dance in Korea also began with nature worship in the very beginnings of the nation. One dance was connected with farming and another with religious services and rituals. Ancient Koreans held services in the sowing season in the fifth lunar month and in the reaping season in the 10th lunar month. They also held other primitive religious rituals in the first and 10th lunar months.

The opening movement of a new arrangement of a traditional court dance called the Flower Crown Dance.

126

Ritual dance includes the *ilmu* or line dance, performed at Confucian shrines and at royal ancestor's shrines, and butterfly dances performed at Buddhist temples. The *ilmu* dance was started by the Koryŏ people. The number of participants in this dance varies according to the importance of the ritual. The most dignified occasions, such as the annual worship before the royal ancestral tablets and the spring and autumn festivals, call for 64 persons, or eight lines of eight persons. An *ilmu* dance is performed by two groups of men in scarlet robes, one representing civil officials and the other, military. Civilian dancers each hold a flute and a feather while the military hold a wooden shield.

There are four types of Budhist dances which have survived to this day. Buddhist dances, as well as music, were intended as supplications for Buddha to permit the souls of the dead to enter Nirvana. The *Nabi Ch'um,* or "Butterfly Dance," is performed by a dancer wearing a long white or

Sungmu, or "The Monk's Dance," a Buddhist dance developed during the early Chosŏn period.

yellow robe, the full sleeves of which represent the wings of a butterfly and trail on the floor behind the red overmantle worn across one shoulder. Another one, the *Mogu Ch'um,* or "Wooden Idol Dance," is a sort of grace before meals. Two dancers, wearing the same costume as in the butterfly dance, circle a white-painted log representing the devil and strike it with gaily decorated mallets. The next one is the *Para Ch'um,* a cymbal dance which involves the manipulation of two large and heavy metal plates that are struck at crucial moments of movement. This dance is perhaps the most difficult and taxing of the Buddhist dances. The last, called *Sŭngmu,* or "Monk's Dance," involves the use of a drum placed on the floor. The dancer, wearing a monk's hood and costume and holding a stick, expresses the human struggle between spirit and flesh, ending in a climactic swirl and an ecstatic bravura of the drum.

Shamanism in Korea is very ancient and is still extant in some rural

128

The fast and furious Nongak, or Farmers' Dance, conveys the vigor and joy of rural life (upper left). The Pŏpko Ch'um (Law Drum Dance) is a variation of a Buddhist dance (left). While the court dancer (above) is known for slow, sedate performances, the shaman (right) portrays ecstacy through highly vivacious dances.

communities. Its rituals, consisting mostly of frenzied dance movement with accompanying music, are intended to exorcise evil spirits, cure diseases, or bring good luck. To perform this dance, the shaman or sorceress, called *mudang*, wears a red stovepipe hat adorned with a feather and carries two fans, yellow and black. The shaman rites involve earthy humor, badinage, and exuberant high spirits. Preparatory to the climax, ending in a trance-like performance, the shaman performs various highly agitated, acrobatic dances, wielding a number of symbolic objects such as spears, knives, and a bell tree. At one of the climaxes of the ritual the shaman dances in her bare feet on the edges of two long sharp swords. Though there must be various rational explanations of how this feat is accomplished, the onlookers regard it as miraculous and a sure sign that the spirit which has been sought has been successfully invoked. Many aspects of the shaman ritual which have aesthetic appeal have been recently adapted as folk dances for entertainment purposes.

129

The traditional dramatic folk dances can be classified into three categories: the mask play, the puppet play and the operatic drama. The mask play was performed during the ninth century during the period of the three kingdoms in connection with agricultural festivals. Later in the Koryŏ Kingdom it became very popular and was developed in the Chosŏn Kingdom, practically as an official function of the court. But in the late Chosŏn period, with the social development of the middle class, it again served for the common people's amusement.

One of the unusual dramas was called *sandae*, after the royal nomenclature for the office responsible for handling mask shows. It was a spectacle off 10 acts and 13 scenes with an official title for each main act and scene. The *sandae* had an all-male cast, playing and dancing to the accompaniment of traditional Korean drums, strings and brass blaring out tunes based on folk songs. It also had one puppet doll and a set of 24 masks, one for each member of the cast. It was performed on a makeshift stage in the open air in the village square on holiday occasions. Original dramas were quite long and, starting after sunset, the show continued deep into the night.

Another popular drama was called the "Five Clowns" and was an acrobatic show. "Five Clowns" was named for the generals who took positions to the north, south, east, west, and center in accordance with the Confucian set of rituals for music and dance. It was performed by village amateurs on the 15th day after the first moon under the direction of an old village man well versed in the play.

The second category of old Korean drama is the puppet play, which is presumed to have existed since the Three Kingdoms period. One of the typical examples was *Kkoktugakshi* which comes from a Mongolian name. The puppet play was performed in the open with no stage. But four pillars were erected in an open space and draped with cloth to make a square enclosure. The musicians sat outside the curtain and played the role of commentators in response to the puppets' dialogue.

Both the puppet plays and the mask plays had the same theme, to satirize the upper classes and Buddhist monks while describing the common people's daily life.

The third category is *p'ansori*, a kind of opera or epic of country music. This singing play was performed in the time of the Chosŏn Kingdom. Originally *p'ansori* came from the sorceress' epic for omen telling, but in the late 18th century it became entertainment for the common people and the stories of *p'ansori* became more realistic, narrating the common people's daily lives. *p'ansori* also needed no special stage, only a straw mat laid down in an open place. A drummer sat beside the singer, making verbal interjections intermittently.

Wooden masks used in a 500-year-old mask dance drama that is still performed in Hahoe, Kyŏngsangbuk-do, where it originated.

Scenes from the Sandae, Pongsan and Kangryong mask dance dramas (opposite page, clockwise from upper left).

130

Primitive Animism and Shamanism

The religion of the ancient Koreans was animistic nature worship. To these ancient people the world seemed full of powers, manifesting themselves in animal and vegetable life, in the heavens above, and in the waters below. Anything which evoked a feeling of awe was revered as being particularly imbued with divine or mysterious power. Therefore, the forces of nature, especially awe-inspiring trees, rocks, or mountains and other inexplicable natural phenomena, became objects of worship. When farmers wished for a good harvest, they held ceremonies which were intended to propitiate the local, limited gods of field and forest.

The community consisted not only of the living, but of the dead ancestors, who were custodians of the source of life and who watched

A shamanistic painting of the Sanshin, or Mountain Spirit (left). A woman pays homage at a shrine for Toksong, the lonely saint (above).

over fertility, sustenance and growth. They were conceived as still active, and showed their approval by giving abundant fertility in plants and animals and success in hunting and harvest.

The shaman himself, called *mudang* in Korea, is a wizard-priest closely akin to the medicine-man. Shamanism is based on the belief that the visible world is pervaded by invisible forces or spirits that affect the lives of the living. The *mudang* has the ability to influence the powers of the spirit by magic ritual, and his gift is hereditary, his own ancestors, now good spirits, being the great assistants to his work. His two chief functions are to perform sacrifice, with which is conjoined the procuring of oracles, and to purify houses after a death, preventing the dead spirit from -continuing his injurious presence among the living. The ceremonies have· a dramatic character, the wizard acting out an ascent to the heavens or a descent to the underworld, and holding colloquy with denizens in scenes of great excitement, ending in an ecstasy and physical collapse.

Even today in some villages, shamanistic prayers are held in spring and autumn for mountain spirits. Also ancestral rituals have been very important to every family in Korea and have become a part of their way of life.

It was during the Three Kingdoms era that more sophisticated religions began to flow into Korea. Taoism, Confucianism and Buddhism came to Korea one after another, and they were readily accepted. They were to stay with the Koreans until modern times. The introduction of advanced religions, however, did not result in the abandonment of shamanistic beliefs and practices. When Taoism, Confucianism and Buddhism entered Korea from continental Asia, none considered itself in conflict with the others, nor in opposition to rites relating to local nature spirits.

One of the strong reasons that animism and shamanism have survived until today in Korea is that Buddhism, which flourished in the Three Kingdoms period and in the Koryŏ Kingdom, was rejected by the Chosŏn Kingdom, as was seen in the review of Korean history. Then the Chosŏn Kingdom adopted Confucianism as the national teaching. This left a gap in the spiritual needs of the common people, because Confucianism was essentially a sane philosophy appealing to the learned society. It could not replace Buddhism which was popular among humble Koreans. Instead, animism and shamanism, ever potent in the countryside, surged in to fill the gap left by the absence of Buddha's potent powers in the supernatural. Thus, the decline of Buddhism during the passage of time meant the increase of animism and shamanism among the general public in Korea.

Changsŭng, or spirit posts, stand guard at the entrance to a village (above). Evidence of lingering shamanist beliefs are these piles of stones at a temple at Mt. Manisan in Chŏllabuk-do.

Some of the relics of prehistoric Korea are very unusual in the history of Korean religion. There are strong indications that the ancient Chosŏn people were a very religious people. As indicated in the Tan-gun legend, the legendary founder of Korea is a grandson of a god. Such a legend was originated in order to make Koreans believe that their national founder was the offspring of the heavenly God. Also, both anthropologists and historians agree on the fact that dolmens, which the ancient Chosŏn people worshiped, and menhirs, to which they prayed for the protection of their community and for proliferation of their offspring, can be found in Korea in larger numbers than in any other part of the Far East. As has been seen, in 5,000 years the Koreans developed their own distinctive ideas concerning man's origin, nature, destiny and his relationship to the universe in which he lived.

Taoism

Taoism is based on the teaching of the *Lao-tzu* or *Tao-te-ching* (Classic of the Way of Power) and the *Book of Chuang-tzu*. The Taoist belief mistrusts an activist philosophy which seeks to control human society, and it stresses attention to ceremony, duty, and public service. A Taoist would rather escape from the attractions of political office and avoid conventional social obligations in order to nourish his own inner life. He longs to lead a simple, spontaneous, meditative life in communion with nature and in obedience to cosmic laws. The teachings of Lao-tzu and Chuang-tzu were brought to Korea in the seventh century, and there were some active efforts to study them. But the strongest imprint of Taoism's influence can be found in the guiding principles of the *Hwarang* elite corps of Shilla, who were trained in patience, simplicity, contentment, and harmony.

Because of the Taoist philosophy that development of civilization is a degradation of the natural order, and their ideal of return to an original purity, Taoism failed to deeply affect government and the general society in Korea. But the most apparent trace of Taoist influence among the Koreans is the search for blessing and longevity, the strongest of the Taoist features. One may observe the indelible Taoist mark in the two Chinese characters, *Su*, longevity, and *Pok*, or blessing or happiness, which are used to decorate so many everyday articles such as spoons and pillowcases. Should one ask an elderly Korean what constitutes the ultimate blessings, the answer will likely be "longevity and happiness." These are the chief objectives of Taoism.

Su (longevity) and pok (happiness) auspicious ideographs from a 10-panel screen (above).

An embroidered pillow end bearing the same ideographs (right).

Confucianism

Confucius, the famous sage of China, was born in the year 550 B.C. His clan name was Kung and he was a native of the state of Lu, a part of the modern-day Shan-tung area. He appeared at the time of a national crisis. The Chou Dynasty had become very corrupt and had fallen into decay, and the practice of most right principles had disappeared. Ministers murdered their rulers, and sons their fathers. Confucius was frightened by what he saw and he undertook the work of reformation.

His teaching was based on an ideal ethical-moral system intended to govern all the relationships within the family and the state in harmonious unity. Confucius considered social relations to be ordained by heaven, and to be made up of five relationships: ruler and subject, husband and wife, father and son, older and younger, and friend and friend. There is dominance on one side of each of the first four, and submission on the other side. The rule should be one of righteousness and benevolence; and the submission one of righteousness and sincerity. Between friends the mutual promotion of virtue should be the guiding principle. It was true that the duties of the general relations were continually violated by the passions of men, and the social state had become an anarchy. But Confucius had confidence in the preponderant goodness of human nature and in the power of example in learning.

His professed disciples amounted to 3,000, and among them were between 70 and 80 whom he described as "scholars of extraordinary ability." The most closely attached of them were seldom long away from

Illustrations from Samgang-haengshildo, *a book about loyal subjects, filial sons and faithful wives compiled in 1431 by Sŏl Sun on the orders of King Sejong.*

A dance performed during a Confucian ceremony held annually in the spring and autumn at the Confucian shrine on the premises of Sŏnggyun-gwan University.

him. They stood or sat reverently by his side, watched the minutest particulars of his conduct, studied under his direction the ancient history, poetry, and rites of their country, and treasured every syllable which Confucius taught. Confucius bequeathed to posterity several books regarded as the basic classics, some of which he reputedly wrote himself, and others of which he edited in definitive form from earlier versions. To these were added many volumes of commentary, some of them purporting to be dialogues between Confucius and his disciples. Confucius and his disciples used to roam the country visiting and advising the dukes and princes on the right way to govern. But Confucius himself was never successful in obtaining a government post to test his theories, living most of his life as a wandering scholar-teacher.

The philosophy of Confucius embraced no consideration of the supernatural, except for an impersonal divine order referred to as heaven, which left human affairs strictly alone as long as relative order and good government prevailed on earth. In this sense, Confucianism was a religion without a god. But as ages passed, the sage and his principal disciples were canonized by later followers, as a means of inculcating their doctrines among simple and common people. However, Confucianism filled the social function of religion at that time.

According to *Samguksagi* (History of the Three Kingdoms), in 372 the Koguryŏ Kingdom established both a national Confucian academy called T'aehak (great school), which was equivalent to a higher educational institution in their capital, Kyŏngdang, and also private Confucian academies throughout the provinces. The curriculum at the national academy consisted of the five classics which are *Shin Ching* (Book of Odes), *Shu Ching* (Book of History), *I Ching* (Book of Changes), *Chun Chiu* (Spring and Autumn), and *Lichi* (Book of Rites).

The martial arts was one of the important subjects at T'aehak, because of the Koguryŏ people's serious concern with national defense. Also through the five classics they were taught the principles of loyalty and filial piety in order to defend their country and to protect their family and homes.

The neighboring kingdom of Paekche had similar institutions at about the same time. It is interesting to note that in 375 the Paekche people used the title *paksa*, meaning "doctor", for those who were well versed

A participant in the Confucian ceremony held at Sŏnggyun-gwan.

in the five Confucian classics. The kingdom of Paekche sent its famous Confucian scholar, Wang In Paksa, to Japan to transmit Confucius' teaching at this time. He carried the *Confucius' Analects* and the *Book of One Thousand Letters* to Japan. There is a monument in Ueno Park in Osaka, Japan dedicated to Wang In Paksa for his influence on the development of Japanese culture.

Shilla received Confucian thought last among the three kingdoms through Koguryŏ and Paekche. However, when Shilla conquered and absorbed the other kingdoms in the seventh century, interest in Confucianism rapidly increased. The guiding principles of Shilla's famed *Hawarangdo,* a system of training young men who held the key positions for uniting the three kingdoms, were based on Confucius' teaching. Among the five objectives of the *Hwarangdo* principles, loyalty, filial piety, fidelity, and bravery are based on Confucius's teaching. In 682 Shilla established Kukhak, a state higher educational institution which offered a nine-year course primarily teaching the five Confucian classics.

The Koryŏ Kingdom was influenced by Confucianism which was the dominant political philosophy of the period. During this period the public educational institutes developed further, the public service examination system was firmly established, and private Confucian schools also flourished. During the middle of the period Confucianism emerged as a major source of social and political wisdom. The major state institute was named Kukchagam and was for training government officials. The school had three major departments, and students were enrolled in different departments depending on the rank of their parents. Their curriculum was based on the five Confucian classics plus military training.

The Confucian tradition, which had exerted a great influence upon the thoughts and education of the Koryŏ Kingdom, influenced the following Chosŏn Kingdom with even greater force. The founder of the Chosŏn Kingdom adopted Confucian teaching as the national religion and based his principles of good government on Confucianism. Consequently, Confucian scholars received royal favors and were given important official positions.

The Chosŏn government reinstalled a civil service examination system to recruit government officials by merit. The examination system, called the *Kwago,* was divided into two branches, one for administrative service and the other for military service. The examinations were held every three years. All the young men were eager to obtain Confucian education in order to prepare for the civil service examination. To be a scholar was synonymous with Confucianism. And also the popularity of these studies caused schools to spring up all over the country. This desire became stronger and stronger, century after century, so that Confucianism became even stronger in Korea than it was in Confucius' own country, China.

In 1398 King T'aejo opened the famous national Confucian academy Sŏnggyun-gwan (mentioned earlier in Chapter II) for the purpose of training the nation's future leaders. In addition the *sodang* private schools were established throughout the country, The *sodang* was a preparatory school for the higher institution. The curriculum consisted of Confucian classics, Chinese and Korean classical literature, and calligraphy. Recitation of classics was the principal method of teaching.

Confucianism was accepted so eagerly and in so strict a form, that the Chinese themselves, as much as any other, regarded Korea as ''the country of Eastern decorum.'' Confucianism in Korea meant a system of education, ceremony, and civil administration. However, the deeply ingrained Confucian mode of manners and social relations is still a major influence on the way Koreans think and act.

Korean Buddhism

Korean Buddhism is an eclectic cultural product which embraces fields of mythology, ancient religions, literature and the arts. While many elements are common to original Buddhism, they are different from those of India and China in many respects.

Buddhism is a religion as well as a philosophy. It grew out of the teaching of Gautama Buddha that suffering is inherent in life and that one can be liberated from it by spiritual enlightenment. As it spread around the world it began to influence philosophies of life, the social structure, and culture as a whole.

Gautama Buddha, who was a self-perfected man, one who had achieved the mind's enlightenment, is the historic founder of Buddhism. Details of his life were not written down earlier than 236 years after his death. Since then they have been preserved variously in the Pali, Sanskrit, Chinese, Tibetan and Korean writings of Buddha's philosophy and life.

Since Buddha is the central figure of Buddhism some of his biography is in order. He was born of the Aryan race, Sakya clan, south of the present day Nepal in the Southern Himalayas, the first son of King Suddhodava Gautama and Queen Maya in the year 563 B.C. The account of his birth is a very interesting one. His parents had been childless for 20 years. One night Queen Maya dreamt of a white elephant entering her womb. After that she found herself with child. As was the custom of her country, she started on the journey to her parents' home to be delivered of the child. On the way, however, at a place called Lumbini Park, she gave birth to a son. He was given the name Siddhartha, which means "every wish fulfilled."

His birth was attended by wise men, interpreted in his land as a good

Some of the images of Buddha in the Thousand Buddhas Hall of Chikchisa, a temple that dates from around 418 (top). Monks leaving a temple's main sanctum after holding daily prayers (above).

omen. They told of this child, ''If he remains in the palace, he will become a great king to rule over the Four Seas. If he leaves, he will become a Buddha, a self-enlightened one, and the world's savior.''

When Siddhartha was 12 years old, he was allowed out of the palace for the first time. Upon returning to the palace he could not regain any peace of mind.

For the first time in his life he began to meditate seriously about life and death. He perceived clearly the evils of disease, old age, wretchedness, sickness and suffering in general. He wondered what life was, who he was, from where he came, to where he was destined, and how human beings could be liberated from all this suffering.

He continued to wonder, to meditate and to ask about these wonderings to his father and his teachers, receiving satisfactory answers from none. His father, the King Suddhodava Gautama, remembered the wise men's predictions and tried every way to induce his son to remain at the palace. But at the age of 30, Siddhartha reached a desperate climax in his years of mental struggles and meditations. He decided to leave the palace and to seek the solutions elsewhere, to try to save himself and the rest of mankind.

He set out to visit the wisest scholars of his day. First he studied under Alara Kalama, a great teacher of Hindu. But he could find no satisfactory answers to the wonderings of his heart. So he went to another teacher, Uddaka, to seek the answers. Again the seeking was in vain. He wandered in search of still another teacher who could give him his answer.

Finally he settled in the town of Uruvilva, where he began his medita-

Sketches of Six Mudra

Do Not Fear

Meditation

Giving

tions for enlightenment. For about six years, he concentrated in his deep thoughts about how to control his mind, practicing asceticism as the main method for his meditations. He gave up the asceticism one day by accepting a bowl of food from a village maiden. His immediate followers became disillusioned and deserted him. However, he stayed under a jambu tree, called the tree of wisdom, until he had found enlightenment.

On December 8, in his 35th year, Gautama found the path of enlightenment and became a buddha, an enlightened one. Some called him Sakyamuni, or the world-honored, blessed one.

Buddhism is a 3000-year-old religion and one of the most comprehensive and profound spiritual achievements in human history. In its earliest form it included one of the finest moral philosophies known to mankind and concerned itself with intellectual development and philosophy, as well as psychology, mysticism, metaphysics, magic, ritual, morality and culture. In every country it exalted the indigenous culture, and it helped produce and influence the great cultures of China, Japan, Tibet, Thailand, and Korea, i.e., the art of the Tang Dynasty of China, the greatest art of the Saiko period in Japan, the period of King Asoka in India, and the Shilla Kingdom of Korea. Throughout the East it has set a standard of tolerance and love of nature. These cultures are altogether beautiful; Buddhism is an integral part of their libraries, gardens, anecdotes, tales and romances of various sorts. The construction of Buddhist temples and pagodas and the publication of scriptures came to be regarded as a symbol of protection for the state against enemy powers. Some countries absorbed the mythological elements which also contained its philosophical and scientific dissertations. As a result, it became not just a religion or a system of philosophy, but a whole culture, embracing all fields of mythology, religion, literature, and the arts.

Buddhists pray night and day on the birthday

Buddha taught humanity, brotherhood, gentleness, and the simple way of life. His task involved making a good person of a man or woman, developing the human nature, and cultivating the character. Later, cultivating one's character became one of the most important points of educational philosophy in Korea. Teaching good personality is seen to be as important as teaching language, art, literature, arithmetic, etc.

Buddhism always places central emphasis on human affairs. All the other world religions are God-centered religions: we are subjects of God, we are created by Him, we are living according to His order, not by our will. Buddhism, however, is a human-centered religion, teaching that it is up to man to make himself better or worse.

Nothingness, selflessness, and self-denial are fundamental principles for the Korean Buddhist. As a Buddhist one should learn, in self-effacement or humility, that he is nothing. This is the first requirement for all the Buddhists.

Buddha also mentioned that, as a follower of his, one should not expect any kind of honor for his services. True learning must be self-learning and the Buddhist, as an enlightened one, should overcome his individuality or should achieve emancipation from ego. It might seem helpful to give

140

Turning the Wheel of the Law

Mudra of Touching the Ground

Cosmic Union of Male-Female Principles

of Sakyamuni, the Historic Buddha.

rewards for good services to the followers as moral boosters. But for a Buddhist this kind of reward is secondary—or not necessary at all. The true rewards should come from an inner desire to help other human beings to attain the Buddha's character.

Regarding the cultivation of virtues, there are four virtues of expression. These are the virtues of (1) care, (2) loving language, (3) sacrifice, and (4) helping. These four virtues are required for making friendships with other people.

There are seven virtues of attitude for the Buddhist student. They are the virtues of (1) interest in others, (2) obeying the law, (3) compassion, (4) perseverance, (5) progressiveness, (6) concentration, and (7) wisdom.

Buddha went on a journey preaching to the people for 45 years. The most important of his teachings concerned the power of thought. He showed how men could control their minds through concentration and meditation. In the first verse of the Dhammapada he said, "All that we are is the result of what we have thought; it is founded on our thoughts, it is made up of our thoughts." When he arrived at the border of Kusinagave Castle, he was stricken seriously ill, and there he died at the age of 80 in 483 B.C.

At the time Buddhism entered Korea in the fourth century, the country was drawing toward the middle of the Three Kingdoms period. Koguryŏ was the first to adopt Buddhism as a royal creed in 372, Paekche the second in 384, and Shilla the last in 528.

Under the royal patronage, Buddhism spread like wildfire in the three kingdoms. Many temples and monasteries were constructed, and hordes of believers were converted. Royal patronage during the Golden Age of the Unified Shilla period produced a magnificent flowering of Buddhist arts and temple architecture.

During the Koryŏ Kingdom, priests became politicians and courtiers. The Buddhist cult eventually attained such power that it was necessary for the king to become a Buddhist monk in order to reign.

When the Mongols invaded Korea in the 13th century, the reaction of the Buddhist-oriented court was to implore divine assistance by undertaking the immense project of carving the entire bulk of Buddhist scriptures onto wooden blocks for printing. This is the so-called *Tripitaka Koreana*, still extant today.

Each country has preserved many volumes of Buddhist scriptures. The *Tripitaka Koreana* was printed in 1237. This monumental work, with well-arranged contents and wooden type, has been preserved. Its publication was an epochal event in the whole history of printing.

The suppression of Buddhism during the Chosŏn Kingdom was not caused by any defect inherent in its teaching but was due to the Yi Dynasty's official policy of supporting Confucianism. During this period the Buddhist priests stood aloof from worldly life. They devoted themselves to the teachings of their master, to studying and teaching scriptures. In the face of suppression by the government, the Buddhists simply maintained their mission and the spirit to protect the nation.

Christianity.

In the first part of the 17th century, the Korean envoys returning from Peking brought home a book entitled *Introduction to Catholic Religion*, and it attracted their countrymen's special attention. In 1783, Yi Sŏung-hun went to Peking to study Catholicism and passed the catechism examination and was baptized with the Christian name of Peter. In the following year, he returned home carrying some religious articles and the Bible, and began to spread the new teaching among learned people. He baptized several other Koreans. However, the new faith suffered successive persecutions in 1785, 1801, 1839, 1846 and 1869. Despite these intermittent persecutions, the Foreign Mission Society of Paris sent missionaries to Korea continuously. Finally the Catholics obtained freedom of worship as a result of treaties of friendship with some of the Western nations in 1882. In 1889 the Catholics held a grand ceremony for the consecration of the Seoul Cathedral.

The interior of Myŏngdong Cathedral, Korea's first Gothic structure which was built in 1898.

A portrait of Kim Tae-gŏn, Korea's first Catholic priest.

The protestant missionary who left his first footprint on Korea in 1832 was German minister Charles Gutzlaff. He was followed by R.J. Thomas, a Scotsman who came to Korea on September 13, 1865. He came back again the following year aboard an American merchant marine ship. The boat sailed up the Taedonggang River, and Thomas distributed Bibles and preached to the people gathered along the riverbanks. This vessel was fired upon by Korean troops near P'yŏngyang and its crew members were killed. Thomas was taken before the magistrate of P'yŏngyang for questioning. He was found guilty of treason and beheaded. The story is that just before the axe fell, the English "man of Christ" gave his Bible to a wrestler who was watching the execution and prayed for the man's soul. Subsequently the wrestler became a Christian.

In 1882, Korea signed its first foreign treaty of friendship with the United States. This opened Korea's doors to Christian faiths. The first two American missionary pioneers, Henry G. Appenzeller (Methodist) and Horace G. Underwood (Presbyterian), arrived at the same time at Inch'ŏn on Easter Sunday of 1885.

Since Christianity developed from Judaism, an ethnic religion, and at the same time, taught universal truths and was based upon the concept of brotherhood, rich or poor, man or woman, all ages, it was readily accepted by the Korean people who believed that they were themselves heaven-descended. Meantime the old decadent Confucianism and Buddhism had somewhat lost their spiritual significance and hope for the people. Both suffered the common fate of all religions exposed to undue temptations and surfeited by material possessions.

Koreans could understand not only the moral lessons of the Bible, but also its historical background. A small nation in the Near East and a small nation in the Far East were surrounded alike by hostile neighbors and experienced many miseries of a similar kind. The exodus led by Moses was the story which expressed Korea's cherished hope of being an independent nation liberated from foreign forces. The tragedy of Jerusalem and the fate of Palestine under the Roman Empire were identified with Korea's own story under the domination of Japan.

The wonderful development of the Korean Christian Church was influenced by several other factors too. One was the strong Korean desire for westernization and modernization. The Christian teachings opened

Ducksoo Presbyterian Church founded 1946.

H. N. Allen

H. G. Underwood   H. G. Appenzeller

the way to understanding modern thought and, especially modern ideas of democracy. In 1885 an American Protestant missionary group began founding modern schools in Korea. For the first time in Korean history Christian missionaries opened up education for everyone. Only a relative handful of upper-class boys were students in the traditional schools in Korea until this time. This was a tremendous social revolution as well as the beginning of a new era for Korean education. Thus Christians introduced Korea to a modern education which included everybody, upper or lower class, rich or poor, even women. They introduced the sciences and humanities, the modern ideas of which awakened the Korean educators to the need to modernize their education. By stressing the spirit of national independence and the dignity of human rights, Christian teaching of these modern ideas laid the foundation for the growth of the democratic spirit for the first time in Korea.

Later on, of the 33 patriots who led the signing of the Declaration of Independence against the Japanese occupation on March 1, 1919, 16 were Protestants. Indeed, Koreas' independence movement was centered around Korean churches and mission schools.

One other area in which Christians exerted a strong influence was that of the social welfare organizations started by the churches. They started nursery schools, homes for orphans, and homes for the poor. Also the churches helped improve social conditions by launching anti-vice campaigns. They built hospitals and churches on military bases as well as in prisons.

The momentum begun long ago still accelerates the development of Korean churches. In general Korean Christian churches have been great contributors to Korean culture, education and social development.

143

Part Four
Customs and Traditions

Clothing

Koreans possess not only a unique culture but also many traditional costumes. The traditional Korean costumes have a history of about 2,000 years and may still be considered the standard. Perhaps the most distinctive thing about Korean dress is that the apparel of both men and women is often white. Korea was once called a nation of white-dressed citizens. White clothes have become a symbol of the Korean people as a result of their deep-rooted religious beliefs. Therefore, especially for religious ceremonies, they most often wear white clothes.

In the traditional men's costumes, wide trousers are worn, bound tightly at the waist and gathered at the ankles by colored bands. Their jackets

A beautiful silk hanbok, or *dress, an elaboarte vest pendant, and a highly embroidered silk purse are among the items Korean brides have traditionally prepared for weddings (left). A family models traditional winter clothes (right).*

are short and loose and are usually fastened by a tie with a single bow. Over the jacket they may wear a long flowing coat which overlaps and is tied on the right side.

Women's dress is somewhat like the men's except that in the old style they wear two pairs of trousers, one shorter than the other, the longer not reaching the ankle and never tied. In modern days, they wear slips as do their Western counterparts. The dress is simple and women nearly always make their own. A very full instep-length skirt is pleated into a band tying under the arms. This skirt is known as a *ch'ima*. Over this is worn a brief jacket, the *chŏgori*, with full, shaped, long sleeves, which

146

fastens on one side with a bow. The women's dress was made to cover as much of the body as possible.

Nowadays, most men in Korea have virtually discarded the traditional Korean costume. This may be because of the inconvenience the traditional Korean costumes poses in everyday activities. Now the traditional costume is reserved only for occasions of festivity, especially the holidays around New Year's Day or Ch'usŏk (Harvest Moon).

The case is very much different with women. Korean women still cling to the traditional Korean style. The majority of Korean women still do not work outside the home. Even the working girl is expected by all to stay at home when she gets married. They feel very comfortable with the traditional ch'ima and chŏgori. Another reason may be found in the intrinsic beauty of the Korean costume and its suitability to their physique. Korean women are rather long of waist and short of leg compared with most Western women. On this point the Korean costumes are particularly fitted to them, for the ch'ima usually hangs from the breasts and hides the long waistline gracefully.

Women's costumes have remained basically unchanged, except for some slight changes or modifications in the length of the chŏgori, the width of its sleeves, the size of the pleats on the ch'ima, and so forth. However, the number of working women is rapidly increasing and they usually prefer the Western styles. In recent years the traditional costumes have begun losing popularity and more Korean women, especially in urban areas, appear more often in Western outfits. Nevertheless, the traditional women's costume is still favored for "dress-up" wear and, therefore, it will be some time before it disappears from the Korean scene, even if the present tendency continues. Entirely different is the case with Korean men's traditional clothes, which are rapidly disappearing.

The hair styles of both the unmarried man and woman were the same until 50 years ago. The hair was divided in the middle of the forehead and braided to hang down the back, so that seen from the back it was

Women demonstrate how silk thread was spun (left) and "ironing" (right) was done in the past.

148

hard to tell whether one was a boy or a girl. But this style showed a clear-cut distinction between the married and the unmarried. The married woman traditionally wore her hair pulled up into a knot at the nape of the neck, while the married man wore his hair knotted on top of his head and covered by a hat.

During the Three Kingdoms period, the women of Koguryŏ wore their hair long over the right shoulder, while the women of the Paekche Kingdom parted theirs in the middle to hang down in two strands. In the Shilla Kingdom, women swung their hair around the neck, and it slid down the front of the body in a long cascade.

By the end of the Koryŏ period, the Mongol influence raised the long, hanging hair up on the head, where it was bound up in a coil, known as the *cchokturi*. The Mongol hairdo became so popular that women of Koryŏ paid high prices for bundles of other women's hair to add to their own. This mode of hair dressing has survived until the present, especially in the northern part of Korea.

Another style known as *nangja* has been preserved until today. This style is presently worn by mostly older women, who consider the permanent wave too girlish. The origin of this style goes back to the Shilla Kingdom. Women of the court officials around the capital city of Kyŏngju knotted their hair into a ball just above the nape of the neck. This style later spread among the population and finally received royal encouragement. By that time, a pin of four to five inches in length made of gold, silver, or precious stones, known as the *pinyŏ*, was thrust into the knot of hair above the nape to serve as a fastener as well as a decoration.

But all this changed. Today the traditional hair styles and dresses are rarely worn by urban Korean men, except for a few, mostly elderly men, who thus adorn themselves for special occasions or holidays. Some folks in the rural areas, on the other hand, wear traditional clothing every day and many others, including children, do so on special occasions.

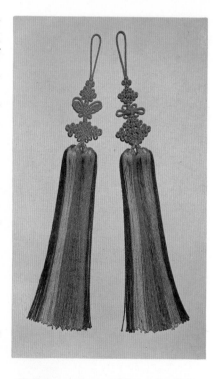

Children dressed in colorful hanbok with traditional hair ribbons (upper left). A variety of hairpins made of gold, white jade and precious stones (top). Norigae, or vest pendants, like these are still worn with hanbok (above).

149

Food

Like most of the people of the Asian continent Koreans have made rice the staple of their diet. One may say that rice is like bread on the dinner table along with their many other dishes such as fish, vegetables, and meat.

Because of Buddhism's influence (Buddhists are vegetarians) over such a long period, vegetables predominate in the Korean diet. Unique local products are mostly vegetable dishes of the home-grown variety as well as mountain-grown. Some popular vegetables are bean sprouts, Korean cabbage, Korean radish, spinach, eggplant, squash, cucumber, and potatoes. Some other typical vegetables are watercress, water lily roots, mushrooms, dandelions, platycodon, fernbrake, lanceolate, lotus root and other wild, edible greens.

The most important meat is beef, and other meats are pork, chicken, rabbit, and pheasant. The meat is roasted or cooked with vegetables to make soup. Most of the dishes are mixtures of meat and vegetables.

Besides vegetables the most important food for Koreans has been seafood. The most widely used fish now are Alaskan pollack and cod. Some of the other typical seafoods are squid, octopus, shark, various kinds

A table set with a regular meal for one person (upper right) and a table set for a special occasion (lower right).

151

of clams, and all kinds of edible seaweed.

The Koreans have a particular liking for strong spices, such as red pepper, garlic, onion, ginger, and sesame and soy sauce.

Among Korean dishes one of the best known is *pulgogi* or "fire-beef", which consists of strips of beef roasted over a brazier at the table after being marinated in a mixture of soy sauce, sesame oil, sesame seeds, garlic, green onions, and sugar. Another favorite dish is *kalbi* or broiled short ribs, that is short ribs cut into about 8-centimeter squares, mixed with the same seasonings as *pulgogi* and cooked similarly. Another dish is *shinsŏllo*, a court dish combining meat or chicken with mushrooms, chestnuts, pinenuts, seafood, leeks, bamboo shoots and other vegetables artistically arranged in a special chafing dish (a brass pot similar to a fondue dish) with glowing charcoal in the lower segment, the food being cooked in the upper. This dish is also seasoned with soy sauce, sesame oil and seeds, garlic, green onions and sugar. Another popular dish is *mandu*, which is similar to egg rolls. Consisting of meat and chopped vegetables wrapped in a flour dough crust, it is steamed, fried, or boiled in water like dumplings. *Mandu* made with pheasant meat is regarded as the best.

Ttŏk, *a sweet made of rice flour and stuffed with a variety of ingredients.*

There are many kinds of cakes. The cake made by mixing rice flour and honey and then boiling it in sesame oil is regarded as one of the highest quality. Most commonly known as *yakkwa*, it has various names, depending upon the shape in which it has been cut. Then there is *tashik* made of such ingredients as chestnuts, green beans, soya beans, the inner bark of the pine tree and pollen from flowers, stirred in honey and boiled.

One food which is unique to Korea is *kimch'i*, a variety of Korean pickled cabbage. This dish is far more important to the Korean diet than anything else. There are almost no other pickle dishes similar to this. Even the word "pickle" can hardly cover the full aspect of *kimch'i*. The chief ingredients of *kimch'i* are Korean cabbage and radish. These are stuffed or mixed with a great diversity of spices and ingredients such as red pepper, ginger, garlic, onion, oysters, fish, meat, chestnuts, pears, etc. *Kimch'i* is for all year round, but it is especially important in the winter when other vegetables are not available. It is an annual function in Korean homes to prepare enough pots of *kimch'i* for the approaching winter. It requires a big expenditure in each household, while at the same time, it gives a pleasant, holiday-like anticipation of abundance during the *kimjang*, or *kimch'i*-making, season. When enough *kimch'i* to last the winter (3-4 months) has been stored safe in huge stone jars, which are 38-76 liter containers, and it has been buried underground outside, every household feels at ease, relieved and safe.

Korean desserts mainly consist of fruits and cold drinks. There are various kinds of fruits available throughout the seasons. Fresh fruits are preferred to cooked or preserved fruits. For the cold drink there is *shikhye*, a sweetened drink made from rice and served with pine-seeds. Another version is made of dried persimmons soaked in ginger water for two or three days and spiced with cinnamon powder when served.

The Korean, as a rule, has three meals a day. Breakfast is customarily considered the principal meal of the day and, therefore, it is not unusual for guests to be invited for breakfast. Lunch is usually simple and often consists of the leftovers from breakfast. The evening meal is almost the same as breakfast, but is conventionally less elaborate than the morning meal.

Foods prepared for holidays and special occasions.

Turnip and Cabbage Kimch'i

Shinsŏllo *and Noodles*

Ttŏk

Yakkwa

Housing

Traditional Korean houses are constructed with heavy square wooden posts set at each corner, resting on dressed corner stones, and supporting large, wood beams, over which round rafters form the ceilings of the rooms. Black roofing tiles are used, resting on a thick bed of earth and kept in place by clay over these rafters. The eaves formed by the exposed ends of the rafters project well beyond the walls on all sides. Such a roof resists both the heat of summer and the cold of winter. This type of black tiled roof was introduced during the Three Kingdoms period and the elaborate roof style has survived until today with slight modification. The intricate arrangement of tiles together with other decorations on the roof serve no utilitarian purpose, but are considered to add grace and dignity to the house. Once the size and intricate adornment of the roof were a kind of measurement of the financial well-being of the family. The walls are filled in with stone, mud, and plaster after the roof is completed. The houses are generally surrounded by stone walls, pierced by two gateways, an outer and inner one.

The main building contains a large center room, which serves as a parlor, at either end of which are smaller rooms for the use of the male members of the family. The women live in inner apartments in accordance with the custom of keeping the sexes apart. These inner apartments consist of three portions; bedrooms, a hall and a kitchen.

The most unique aspect of a Korean house is the heating arrangement, called *ondol*. This type of heating under the floor was started during the Three Kingdoms period. The system was gradually developed and modified to suit the conditions and requirements of the Korean people. By the middle of the Chosŏn Kingdom, about 350 years ago, it was established firmly. A Korean house without *ondol* is very rare. This holds true even for those houses which are of Western style.

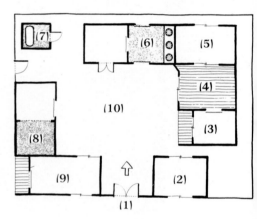

(1) *Taemun*: main entrance
(2) *Kŏnnŏnbang*: spare room
(3) *Kŏnnŏnbang*: spare room
(4) *Maru*: hall with wooden floor
(5) *Anbang*: women's quarters
(6) *Puŏk*: kitchen
(7) *Hwajangshil*: toilet
(8) *Oeyanggan*: stable
(9) *Sarangbang*: men's quarters
(10) *Anmadang*: inner courtyard

The floor of a room equipped with *ondol* is made of slabs of granite stone, rough cut, about 30 by 45 centimeters and about 5 centimeters thick, supported on rows of stone or brick forming the smoke flues. They are all laid in mud or clay mortar. Over the rough stone slabs is a layer of beaten clay or cement worked to a smooth flat surface. Two or three layers of newspapers are pasted over it and then a layer or two of Korean paper. Finally a layer of heavy, oiled paper is pasted over the foundation, and vegetable oil or varnish is applied on the oil paper. The finished floor is tight, smooth and hard, through which flue gases will not escape unless the clay or cement underneath is shrunken, cracked or warped by overheating.

The fireplace is usually located in the kitchen, where wood is fed into the fire, which sends out heat through a flue to the *ondol* and, at the same time, cooks the food. Thus *ondol* is an efficient method of utilizing fuels. In recent years, firewood has become expensive, besides which the government has banned the cutting of trees. As a result, the traditional structure of the *ondol* was slightly modified to use inexpensive coal in place of firewood.

Today, however, it would be difficult to point out a typical Korean house. Nearly all recent houses are concrete or ferro-concrete structures. Though not widely recognized, this change, from predominantly wood structures

A large traditional style Korean house (left). The interior of the sarangbang, or men's quarters (lower left), and the interior of the anbang, or women's quarters.

to predominantly concrete structures, entails a subtle, yet far-reaching change in the Korean lifestyle. Many Koreans in big cities have taken to living in Western-style houses or apartments. But still many urban houses and almost all of those in the countryside embody the traditional style.

In most traditional homes, the Koreans sit on the floor; they do not use chairs. Bedrooms and dining rooms are not specially distinguished, so that usually a living room also functions as a dining room.

There is some uniqueness in the interior decoration and gardening of the average Korean homes. The traditional interior decorations call for scrolls of paintings or calligraphy to be hung over the walls, with folding screens of paper or silk paintings set in the corners of the rooms. And the large, long pillow with embroidery decorations is placed on the floor to serve as a kind of arm-rest. Such articles, bearing paintings and calligraphic works of sophisticated tastes, have been considered as adding dignity to the living areas. Gardening was developed in the royal palaces and residences of a few high-class members of the court. But now most Koreans love flower gardens and wherever they can locate the space, they plant these as well as build Oriental rock gardens. It is an attempt to re-create the effect of steep mountains and deep valleys as nature has created them.

155

Lifestyle

A baby used to be born in its mother's room. However, for a first child, an expectant mother would go to her own mother's house for its birth. Nowadays more and more women go to maternity hospitals for delivery. To recuperate after the birth of a child, a mother is served seaweed soup and rice. In the old days, it was customary to hang a string across the gate post and, in the case of a baby boy, pieces of charcoal and red peppers were fastened to it. In the case of a girl, pieces of charcoal and green pine branches were hung on the string. No visitors, even relatives, were allowed to visit a house for three weeks after the birth. After three weeks the string was removed.

A kŭmjul, or straw rope, strung across a gate indicates the birth of a child (above). A child celebrates his tol, or first birthday (right).

Normally the head of the family or the oldest living person in the family provided a name for the child. Koreans consider that the name is so important that one's future success will depend upon his name. Korean names almost universally have three parts. The family name or surname is placed first, and the middle and last name put together can have a special meaning as well as identify the generation.

On the 100th day after the birth of a child, a big celebration is held, even today. If the child is the first and male, the party is especially elaborate. Many varieties and large quantities of food are prepared and

Young girls learn tea making and drinking etiquette.

a large number of guests are invited. Due to the high infant mortality rate occuring in olden times during the first 100 days from birth, a child reaching its first 100 days was given a special ritualistic celebration, a custom which still prevails today.

Home life of the Korean people has been based on Confucius' teaching. One of the most influential codes of ethics in family life has been filial piety. The grandparents or parents are considered superior at home, and one must pay absolute obedience and reverence to them. In the Korean home obedience and courtesy have been accorded the utmost importance. As outmoded as the teaching may be thought by some, it still contains important elements applicable to present-day Korean home life.

The majority of Korean mothers stay home and take the responsibilities of home education for their children. Korean parents are greatly concerned with each families' traditions that are inherited from their ancestors. They try to hand these down to the children. Moral education and instruction on good behavior are the most important elements of home education until children reach the age of seven, when they go to elementary school. Throughout the childhood and teenage years the mother is tolerant and makes a total sacrifice for her children, while the father remains a strict disciplinarian.

During the young adult period, both males and females have various restrictions, especially females. One of the Confucian ethical codes of conduct used to dictate the iron rule that "male and female shall not sit close after the age of seven." This rule has long ceased to apply, but its lingering influence still demands many restrictions on young people. Most parents still do not allow their children to date until they are of college

A traditional wedding ceremony.

age. Some conservative families do not allow dates even until marriage. When young people reach the marriagable age (between 20 and 30 years of age), the wedding takes place after a period of engagement.

The primary characteristic of the history of the marriage system in Korea is parental arrangement, which is deep-rooted in a society based on Confucian teaching, under which the head of the family has the absolute authority over his family members. One aspect in the evolution of the marriage system reflects the transition from the arrangement of marriage by others, without regard to the wish or intention of the parties concerned. The purpose of marriage in Korea in the old times was not related to individual happiness in the contracting parties, but rather was intended to secure the succession of lineage and the prosperity of the family. The choice of one's future husband or wife and the decisions of the whole event of the wedding were entirely up to the parents.

The most interesting phenomenon of the marriage system at the present time in Korea is that the traditional marriage through parental arrangement is still popular with the slight modification that even though parents make the arrangement, the final choice is up to the individual young people involved. In recent years, even in arranged marriages, young men and women have a certain period of dating after they are introduced to each other by the intermediaries, which constitutes a sort of compromise in the traditional pattern. The Western-style marriage based on love is becoming more frequent in the urban districts and is expected to increase. Presently about half of the marriages in the country are presumed to result from romances.

The traditional wedding ceremony is a colorful event. The groom,

158

A bride in a traditional wedding costume (left). A colorfully clad bridegroom takes his bride home after the nuptials in the enactment of an ancient custom (above).

wearing the wedding hat, coat, belt, and shoes, rides on a brightly decorated horse to the house of the bride. Then the groom must wait outside the bride's house until he is invited in by one of the bride's family members. After some waiting outside the bride's house, the groom is finally admitted, followed by the wedding chest carrier and the groom's family. The wedding chest carrier, who carries gifts to the bride, usually has his face painted black or in other bright colors to play the role of a clown to elicit laughter from the people.

The bride, heavily made up with face powder and rouge and dressed in the traditional wedding costume of a yellow and blue coat with a red or pink skirt, greets the groom and his family with deep bows. Next the couple exchanges vows of eternal devotion to each other with the ceremonial sipping of wine. Then the wedding feast begins. One interesting custom is that toward the end of the feast, the friends of the groom hang him upside down from the beam of the house and make-believe tortue is conducted on the groom by friends who beat the soles of his feet with a stick, demanding money for another big feast. The bride's parents try to remedy the situation as quickly as possible in order to relieve the "torture."

After much feasting the bride and groom retire to the bridal chamber for their first night, with the mischievous friends and neighbors still hovering at the door of the chamber to peek at the couple and generally to harass them in a congenial way.

After the wedding the groom stays for three days with his bride at her house before he can take her to his house in the palanquin. Then the entire wedding ceremony is repeated again with the groom's relatives and

159

The 60th birthday is a very special occasion when one receives bows from children,grandchildren and relatives and is treated to a sumptuous feast.

neighbors at his parent's home.

In recent years people have tended to choose a less elaborate ceremony performed in a more modern style. Christians usually observe the ceremony at a church, while many use commercial "wedding halls," or even hold the ceremony at a big restaurant. The costumes of the modern-style wedding are similar to Western wedding costumes and a Western style reception may follow too. However, after the modern wedding ceremony, there are still the traditional nuptial bows to the groom's parents and family and the drinking of ceremonial wine by the couple.

After the wedding, the newly-wed couple usually live in the same house with the husband's parents. Therefore, sometimes three generations live under the same roof. As a wife, the Korean woman is expected to lead a life of modesty and absolute virtue. Again this idea is from the Confucian teaching that the wife's first principle is obedience, then faithfulness, and finally cooperation.

The majority of Korean housewives still rely on their husbands for the economic support of the family. However, in recent years, increasingly larger numbers of housewives who are college graduates are endeavoring to engage in both housekeeping and an outside career.

Another special feature of Korean home life is that grandparents are often living under the same roof. It is almost unthinkable to send them to nursing homes or to have them live separately. Grandparents play an important role in guiding young children to learn and to carry on the family traditions.

An important event in any Korean's life is *hwan-gap*, or the 60th birthday. As a matter of fact, this is the day when one has completed one's zodiacal cycle. This is no doubt an auspicious occasion, but the real reason for its importance in the past may have been the fact that not many people lived that long. On this day, one dresses up in the best possible clothes, is offered the richest food and drinks, and receives best wishes for

longevity and felicity from children and grandchildren. Relatives and acquaintances are invited to a grand banquet. The number of guests present at the ceremony and festivities used to be regarded as an indication of one's social standing, although the present trend is to observe *hwangap* in a small, private gathering.

The funeral is another important ceremony, and every man of filial piety, assisted by his relatives and close friends, buries a parent with the greatest respect. From the day of death until burial, breakfast and supper are served for the dead, the food being what the departed one liked most during his or her lifetime. On arrival at the selected burial ground, a last parting ceremony is conducted and the body is interred, cremation being very rare. The choice of the burial ground requires very careful inspection, and the decision is made after many consultations with geomancers and priests. When the burial is finished a tablet made of chesnut wood in memory of the dead is brought to the home and enshrined in the family shrine. The period of mourning ranges from three months to three years according to the degree of the relationship. For a father or a mother it is three years, but if the mother dies before the father, then one year. All members of the house pay a visit to the burial ground on holidays, especially on Tano in the spring and Ch'usŏk in the fall.

While the custom is fast disappearing, the bier was traditionally carried to the burial site with much fanfare.

Part Five
A Tour of the Ten Most Beautiful Wonders of Korea

Seoul

Seoul, the capital of Korea, is one of the world's ten largest and most compact cities. The city nestles below a low mountain ridge with a population of over nine million. The Han-gang River, to the south, flows in a westerly direction to the Yellow Sea, physically dividing the city into two sections, the older section on the north bank and the newer suburbs on the south.

Seoul came to claim a place in the history of the nation in 18 B.C. when it became the capital of the Paekche Kingdom. But for a permanent base, Seoul was selected as the royal capital of the Chosŏn Kingdom (1392-1910). The site was chosen for a combination of political, military and superstitious reasons. This central part of the country is obviously the best area from which to administer the whole peninsula. Even the previous dynasty had recognized the importance of this area and maintained a separate palace here. Therefore, Seoul has had an opportunity to preserve much of its intriguing cultural heritage and the many sagas of its rich past.

For both the serious student of Korean history and the casual sightseer there is, in Seoul, a wealth of lore and knowledge about Korea and its people. There are few cities in the world, much less capitals, where the very new and the ancient exist side by side in perfect harmony. The city's past glories are best displayed by its stately ancient palaces such as the Kyŏngbokkung Palace with its ten-story Koryŏ pagoda, and the Folklore Museum and Ch'angdŏkkung Palace to the east, with Naksŏnjae, the residence of the few remaining members of royalty, Tonhwamun Gate and Piwon, or the Secret Garden, with its many pavilions, ponds and bridges.

Today Seoul is a fully modern metropolis with many first-class Western-style hotels. English is spoken at many shops, hotels and restaurants. Just a few steps from the major hotels in the center of the city is Tŏksugung Palace. It includes two Western-style buildings constructed in the early part of this century which stand near the ancient tile-roofed throne hall and annex buildings where the king once received foreign envoys, an example of Seoul's unique blend of old and new. Ch'anggyŏnggung, next to Ch'angdŏkkung Palace, has been restored recently.

Seoul's special lure and charm are its palaces with their traditional, classic architecture, representing Korea's colorful history. For the average tourist on a tight schedule, a half-day visit to one of the palaces will be highly rewarding. The palaces are the most obvious sightseeing attractions in the capital and fortunately all are conveniently located near the downtown center. For a brief moment a visitor may catch glimpses of Korea's heritage from the worn stone paths, intricately patterned murals, and from the clay figures which sit on roof ridges in eternal vigilance, warding off evil.

An islet in the Han-gang River, Yŏŭido is the site of numerous government and semi-governement buildings as well as a chic apartment district.

Kŭnjŏngjŏn, the main throne hall of Kyŏngbokkung.

Kyŏngbokkung Palace

In 1394, King T'aejo, who founded the Chosŏn Kingdom, began building Kyŏngbokkung Palace in order to move his government from Kaesŏng. The construction work was completed in the following year and the king's government moved into the newly constructed palace on October 28.

The palace was destroyed during the Japanese invasion in 1592. Its reconstruction was undertaken by the Prince Regent Taewon-gun in 1865 and completed two years later. Most of the interior parts of the reconstructed palace were destroyed by the Japanese again in 1910 and today there remains only a limited part of the palace structure.

The 13-story pagoda standing in the garden of the palace today formerly belonged to the Kyŏngch'ŏnsa Temple. During the Japanese occupation the pagoda was removed to Japan. It was not until 1960 that the ancient pagoda was recovered by Korea and reset at its present location. The pagoda is set on a three-story star-shaped pedestal and has a ten-story stone structure which was built in 1348 during the Koryŏ Kingdom. The pagoda has refined engravings which lend magnificent beauty to the whole stone structure.

The Kŭnjŏngjŏn Hall of the Kyŏngbokkung Palace served as the place where coronation ceremonies and other official events were held. The

Kyŏnghoeru

Kyŏngch'ŏnsa Pagoda (ten story stone pagoda).

168

Hyangwonjŏng

front garden of the hall is lined with stones with inscriptions depicting the ranks of court officials.

The Kyŏnghoeru Pavilion served as a place of banquets hosted by the king. This pavilion is a two-story banquet hall set in an artificial pond with two stone bridges leading to the hall on the east and a stone staircase serving as a gangplank. The pavilion is surrounded by stone railings on which are carved a diversity of animal figures, as in the throne hall. Forty-eight large tapered columns of white granite support the superstructure from the lower platform; the superstructure has an inner and an outer veranda with sliding doors between. The lower story is open and the upper story provides a spacious wooden floor with three stages, the central stage being higher than the others. A great curving roof caps the structure. Located to the northeast of this pavilion is the Hyangwonjŏng Pavilion whose beauty is especially evident in the spring and autumn. To the north of Hyangwonjŏng is the National Folklore Museum. It stands on the former site of Kŏnch'onggung, the hall where Queen Min was murdered by Japanese hoodlums on the eve of the collapse of the Chosŏn Kingdom.

The Sajŏngjŏn Hall served as the king's office and later the meeting hall of the king's cabinet. The king also handled administrative matters daily in this hall. Kyŏngbokkung is the oldest, largest and most important of the fine palaces in Seoul.

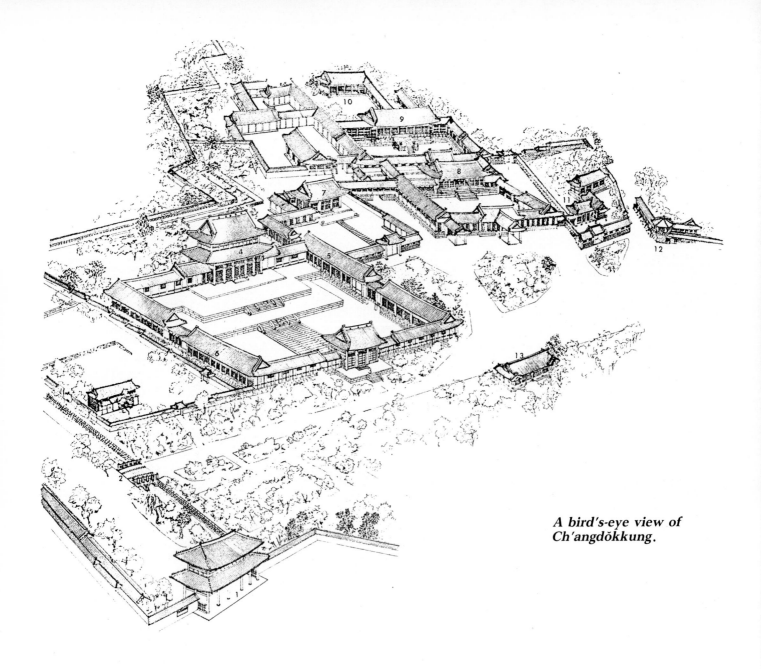

A bird's-eye view of Ch'angdŏkkung.

Ch'angdŏkkung Palace

This palace was built in 1405 by King T'aejong, the third monarch of the Chosŏn Kingdom. It was burnt by the invading Japanese troops in 1592, but the Tonhwamun Gate, the main entrance, fortunately escaped. This gate, therefore, stands out as representative of wooden architectural work of those days. The Injŏngjŏn Hall is the main hall of this palace which houses various pieces of furniture such as imperial chairs and a throne of magnificent proportions. To the northeast is Sŏnjŏngjŏn Hall, in the front garden of which stood the Sŏnjŏngmun Gate. The hall was the resting place of the king. To the east of this building is the small pavilion of Hŭijŏngdang, behind which is the Taejojŏn Hall. This hall served as the living quarters of the king and queen.

This palace takes up 31 hectares and is the largest and the only entirely traditional example of the royal residences. The home of 13 successive Chosŏn kings, its stately typical Korean buildings contain mementoes of the last dynasty, including many rooms furnished just as they were when the king's family and their courtiers lived there. The royal coach and early motor cars used by the royal family are preserved in Ch'angdŏkkung.

170

Injŏngjŏn, the throne hall of Ch'angdŏkkung.

Ōsumun Gate and Chuhamnu

Kwallamjŏng Pavilion

Adjacent to the palace is the famous Piwon or Secret Garden, a fairyland of intertwining paths linking wooded slopes, lotus ponds and pleasure pavilions. This garden reflects the typical Korean beauty of a dozen arbors, and some lovely ponds in the garden give one the feeling of entering a wonderland. One can easily spend the whole day in complete wonderment. Strolling through the garden along the sloping paths and trails, one is astonished by the quaint pavilions, all attended with tales hundreds of years old. The gardens, landscaped in 1623 for royal recreation, are famed for their magnificent natural beauty. One of the most fascinating features of the gardens is a square lotus pond with curious pavilions around it. One will notice here, for example, the Puyongjŏn Pavilion with its two pillars submerged in the water. This 20-sided pavilion is known today as one of the world's finest examples of pure geometrical design.

In a secluded garden across the street from the palace lies Chongmyo, housing the ancestral tablets of Chosŏn's Yi Dynasty kings and their queens. It is here that one can visualize the pomp and ceremony of the Confucian style memorial services held five times yearly during the Chosŏn period. Recently the ceremonies have been revived and are reenacted every year by descendants of Chosŏn's royal Yi family to keep alive the culture of this period. Traditional colorful costumes and musical instruments are used in this ceremony.

173

Chunghwajŏn, the throne hall of Tŏksugung.

Tŏksugung Palace

The palace buildings and the gardens situated between the old capitol building and South Gate in the center of the city contain both the true, traditional style, Chosŏn buildings and some excellent ones with a modern Western touch. Nearly all of the buildings on the grounds have some sad history. It was in this palace that the 500 years of the Chosŏn Kingdom drew to a painful and tragic end as a result of the Japanese occupation in 1910. Tŏksugung was originally built in the 15th century as a detached palace for Prince Wŏlsan who was passed over twice for the throne. He was loved and respected by all and was an avid reader and patron of the arts. The main buildings were built on a small scale. However, the stone building, designed by an English architect, was an addition. This palace is now one of the most popular parks, since it has a lovely garden and is located in the heart of the city of Seoul.

The Seoul City Wall and Gates

The capital city is encircled by four mountains, Mt. Naksan to the east, Mt. Inwangsan to the west, Mt. Namsan to the south and Mt. Pukhansan to the north. The wall surrounding the city was built in 1398 and has a total length of 16 kilometers.

Construction of the gates began in 1395 as part of the wall reconstruction and was completed in 1398. The present Namdaemun, or South Gate, was reconstructed in 1447 and is now the oldest wooden structure in Seoul. The gracefully curved lines of the double eaves and the protruding round beams of the gate give the imposing structure a feminine beauty. Tongdaemun, or the East Gate, is still standing on the original site. A characteristic of the East Gate is its vase-shape and double stone walls. The shape and double wall structure were designed for easy defensibility from attacking enemies.

The gates were opened and closed with the sound of a bell in the morning and evening. It is said that the gates were opened at three in the morning and closed at four in the afternoon.

*Namhansansŏng,
an ancient fortress
in the southern
outskirts of Seoul.*

Games of the 24th Olympiad Seoul, 1988

"HODORI"
1988 Olympic Mascot

Harmony and Progress is the motto for the 1988 Seoul Olympic Games. The Games are set to run from September 17 through October 2, 1988.

At the 1988 Olympics, official competitions will be held in 23 sports and demonstration games in two others. Of the official sports, tennis and table tennis are new additions to the Olympic Games.

The Seoul Sports Complex (left) will be the main venue for the 24th Olympics.

Seoul Vicinity

Folk Village

A traditional Korean folk village is located 30 minutes south of Seoul near Suwon, and it reenacts the enchanting rural life in Korea of hundreds of years ago.

An old gentleman with a slender bamboo pipe in hand and wearing a wide-brimmed horsehair hat strolls under the low eaves of a straw-thatched home. On a wooden-floored porch, a woman is ironing clothes by beating them with two clubs, while in the next courtyard another housewife is spinning silk thread from a small white cocoon simmering in a pot of boiling water.

This village was erected in 1973 and now includes aspects of almost everything uniquely Korean from days gone by. Homes typical of the various provinces of Korea can be identified. In the village square farmers dancing, tight-rope walkers, old traditional style weddings, funeral processions, kite-flying contests, and graceful dance troupes are seen regularly. The blacksmith, carpenter, potter, and instrument craftsmen can be seen at work in their shops. A *yangban*'s (aristocrat's) house, a watermill and the neat yet humble farmer's home can be entered and their furnishings inspected.

This village is not only a museum of how things might have been but is a living, functioning community showing how things really were. A marketplace has various food shops selling district or regional variations in foods and wines. At the present time the village has exact replicas of 68 exhibitions of the Chosŏn period lifestyle.

A bird's-eye view of the Folk Village (below) where the enactment of traditional wedding (upper right) and other ceremonies can be observed along with workmen making knives (lower right) and other items using ancient methods and techniques.

Kanghwado Island

Historic Kanghwado Island is located in the estuary of the Han-gang River north of Inch'ŏn Port. The driving time from Seoul to the island is about one and a half hours. This is the fifth largest island in Korea and is rich in history as well as natural beauty. Chŏndŭngsa, the island's largest temple and also one of the 30 major temples in Korea, is located here.

The entire spectrum of Korean history from the hazy era of Tan-gun, the legendary founder of the nation, to the time of the opening of Korea to the Western world, can be observed and studied on this island. In the 12th century Korean celadon pottery reached its highest level of artistic distinction and one of the major kilns of the era is located on Kanghwado.

Numerous fortresses were constructed along the mainland side of the island. A wall was built across the ridges of Mt. Munsusan. Remnants of these fortifications seen today date from the mid-13th century, when the Koryŏ king fled to this island from the capital during the Mongol invasion.

A short distance west of Kanghwa City, amid fields of ginseng, lies a prehistoric dolmen. Tan-gun, the founder of this nation, paid tribute to the heavens at the Ch'ŏmsŏngdan Altar, which is located on the islands highst peak, Mt. Manisan. On the summit of this mountain Tan-gun is said to have first established an altar for worship in 2333 B.C.

Also on the southern part of the island is the famed temple of Chŏndŭngsa. Circumscribing the temple grounds is a 1.6-kilometer-long fortress wall which was first built, according to legend, by the three sons of Tan-gun. Many elegant pines, gingko, and flowering cherry trees grace the slopes near the temple. It is believed that one temple on this island was first built during the early Three Kingdoms period when Buddhism was first introduced to the peninsula. However, another temple came into prominence during the late Koryŏ era when King Kojong commissioned the carving of the famous 81,258 wood blocks to print the *Tripitaka* in order to aid in driving out the invading Mongols. King Kojong died while taking refuge on this island, and his grave can still be seen near Kanghwa City. In 1299 the grandson of King Kojong donated a rare jade lamp to this temple, thus giving the temple its name of Chŏndŭng, which means "Inherited Lamp."

Ginseng (below) is one of Kanghwado's major agricultural products.

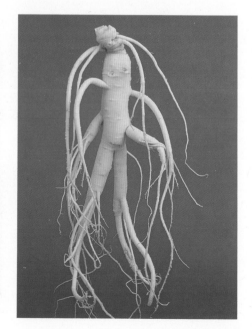

Kanghwado abounds in historic sites such as the Ch'ŏmsŏngdan Altar (above), Chŏndŭngsa Temple (left) and Ch'ojijin (far left).

Kyŏngju

Kyŏngju, 370 kilometers southeast of Seoul, was the capital of the Shilla Kingdom which unified Korea for the first time some 1,300 years ago. UNESCO recognized the global historical significance of Kyŏngju by naming the city one of the world's ten most historic sites.

Kyŏngju is literally a museum without walls and is filled with historic and aesthetic remains of the ancient Shilla Kingdom: Tumuli Park and some 20 ancient tombs, among them O-nŭng, Muyŏl's Tomb, and Kwaenŭng Tomb; Ch'ŏmsŏngdae, or "Star Tower," a stone observatory; Posŏkchŏng, a pleasure garden with a small stone channel in the shape of an abalone shell; Panwolsŏng Castle, the principal royal residence; and Anapchi Pond, another pleasure spot which, when drained, revealed a veritable treasure of Shilla artifacts.

In the Kyŏngju National Museum, the unique golden helmet crowns, artistically shaped golden jewelry, and ceramics and decorations taken from the nearby great earthen tombs of Shilla kings and queens are exhibited. On the grounds of the museum is the bronze Divine Bell of Great King Sŏngdŏk, or the Emille Bell as it is more commonly known, which is the second largest in the world.

The two supreme treasures of Kyŏngju are Pulguksa Temple, located only a few kilometers from town, and Sŏkkuram Grotto Shrine, 8 kilometers up the mountain from the Pulguksa Temple, famous for its seated Buddha statue and carved friezes, all considered pinnacles of Buddhist art.

Ancient Tombs

The legends of ancient Shilla echo across the years, leaving a legacy of beauty and mystery throughout Kyŏngju Valley, where mound-like clusters of ancient tombs, large and small, are located, some 200 in the city proper and 100 outside the city. These mounds vary greatly in size, the largest being as big as a hillock.

Some 2,000 years ago, it was a common custom to bury the dead along with their personal belongings, including gold and silver. In some areas in the northern peninsula underground cells were built in which the dead of a family were placed one after another. And some tribal nations buried their king with all his subordinates alive with him. This custom was observed in Shilla, too, where the sovereign was buried along with ten living men and women. However, this custom of burying people alive was prohibited in 502. Still, the ritual of burying the possessions of the dead continued throughout the following dynasties.

In the Three Kingdoms period the interior hall of a nobleman's tomb was built of stone or timber, and the outer part was covered with stone or clay. The whole tomb was shaped into a semi-globular mound. In the interior were placed personal belongings, daily utensils, and jewelry. On the walls were pictures of processions, banquets, dancing, hunting, and similar activities which showed the ancient customs and culture.

The dead were buried in tombs whose size corresponded to their social standing and wealth. Of the tombs dotting the Kyŏngju area, some are of royalty, some are of aristocrats, and others are of commoners. There were 56 Shilla rulers, but archeological investigation has identified only 36 royal tombs.

Among tombs excavated to date, the Golden Crown Tomb contained the largest quantity of burial objects. Located opposite the hill called

The Tumuli Park in Kyŏngju (above) and the interior of the Heavenly Horse Tomb that has been made into a museum (left).

Ponghwangdae (Phoenix Hill) south of the city, the tomb amazed the archeological world with its wealth of precious items. The findings from the tomb include 59 crescent jades, 30,000 gems of various kinds, 29 gold and silver bracelets, 16 gold and silver rings, one set of four earrings, one gold crown ornamented with no fewer than 67 pieces of jade, five pendants, and two pairs of gold bronze shoes.

Pulguksa Temple

Mt. Tohamsan was thought of by the people of Shilla as a place where benevolent spirits resided. On the mid-slope of Mt. Tohamsan there is a group of magnificent buildings making up Pulguksa Temple, the most superb embodiment of Shilla architecture, sculpture, and craftsmanship.

First built during the reign of King Pŏphŭng (514-540), Pulguksa, "Temple of the Buddha Land," is one of the most famous temples in Korea. Its renown comes not from its age or size but from its beauty as a splendid example of Shilla architecture in a spectacular hillside setting. It also enshrines some of the country's and Korean Buddhism's most important national treasures. Kim Taesŏng, the architect credited with reconstructing this stone master work, in 751 also supervised the construction of the nearby Sŏkkuram Grotto, an annex to Pulguksa and one of Buddhism's most celebrated shrines.

All the wooden structures of Pulguksa Temple were burned to ashes during the Japanese attack in 1593, and what now remains of this temple is said to be only one tenth of its original scope.

Two stone bridges lead to the elevated temple grounds. The one to the east is called the Bridge of Blue Cloud and White Cloud, and to the west is the Bridge of Lotus Flower and the Seven Treasures.

Crossing the bridges, one approaches the main hall through Chahamun Gate, or "Gate of a Purple Mist," because a purple mist settled at the gate of worship in front of the image of Buddha and its granite steps connected with the ground. There are 33 stone steps in the bridges and this design represents the 33 heavens of Buddhism.

In the front yard are two famous stone pagodas, one on each side. The one to the east side is called Tabot'ap (Pagoda of Many Treasures), and the one to the west, Sŏkkat'ap (Pagoda of Buddha).

The Pagoda of Many Treasures, rated as the finest masterpiece of its kind and executed in the Unified Shilla period, surpasses all in originality of form, exquisiteness of composition, and refinement of craftsmanship. The pedestal part, with a staircase on each of the four sides, supports the 10.4-meter-tall granite structure. Its first story consists of five pillars, one in the center and one at each corner. Eight short pillars surround the main body of the octagonal second story, all ringed by a four-cornered balustrade. The third story is surrounded by eight small pillars cut in the shape of bamboo poles, edged in by an octagonal balustrade. The fourth story comprises eight elaborately carved pillars. The octagonal roofstone curves gracefully downward. The pagoda also possesses rich symbolism. The four stairways, one on each side, invite people from all corners of the earth to mount the path of spiritual ascent. The four coarse pillars stand for man in his unrefined state, reaching for the Four Noble Truths of Buddha, represented by the square platform above. He then becomes finer in character, advancing upward through the octagon of the Eightfold Path and eventually to perfection, as shown by the round lotus blossom. The eight-sided wheel of Buddhist law acts as a shield until the spirit ultimately rises above worldly attachments and enters the sublime status of complete purity.

The Pagoda of Buddha, measuring 8.2 meters in height, is a three-story structure resting on a double pedestal, wide and secure. There are no decorations, either on the pedestal or on the main body of the building. Simple, well-balanced, and dynamic, this pagoda embodies masculine beauty, while the Pagoda of Many Treasures imports a feeling of feminine beauty. These structural differences also represent different symbolic meanings. While its companion portrays the process of ascension, this

184

The facade of Pulguksa Temple.

pagoda stands for descent to the earthly world. Eight lotus pedestals, level with the ground, are believed to be seats for Buddhist angels. Simple, strong and masculine, the pagoda represents a type not native to Shilla, but to its western neighbor, the Paekche Kingdom. Standing together, one on either side of the inner court of the temple, the gracious intricacy of the one complements and balances the plain simplicity of the other.

There is an interesting legend surrounding these two pagodas of the Pulguksa Temple:

In the reign of King Kyŏngdŏk (the 35th Shilla monarch), the reconstruction of the Pulguksa Temple was begun in 751. Skilled masons were

brought from far and wide. One of the most renowned was a man named Asadal, from the Paekche region of the Unified Shilla Kingdom. Asadal was commissioned to design and build the twin pagodas in front of the main hall of Pulguksa. His young and lovely wife whom he had recently married was left at home. Asadal missed his wife a great deal and worked long hours in order to return home the sooner. He finally completed the Tabot'ap Pagoda and began work on the Sŏkkat'ap Pagoda. One night a vision of his lovely and patient wife loomed before his eyes. In his vision, she was standing forlornly by a pond near Pulguksa Temple anticipating his return.

Unknown to Asadal, his wife Asanyŏ had made the difficult journey from their home to meet her husband. When she finally reached Pulguksa Temple, the gatekeeper had refused to let her enter. She was told that she could not see her husband while he was working on the important holy mission of building these great pagodas.

She was told that if she went to the Yŏngji (Shadow Pond) she would see the reflection of the great pagoda and her husband. With a heavy heart

Sŏkkat'ap Pagoda

186

Tabot'ap Pagoda

she went to the pond and gazed intently upon the surface of the water. She finally found the reflection of the Tabot'ap Pagoda but could not see the shadow of her husband. She waited and waited for many days in vain. Thinking that her husband would never return, one day she plunged into the pond calling his name.

When Asadal learned about what had happened to his wife he went to the pond and mourned for many weeks. One day he thought he saw his wife on the opposite shore flitting through the trees. He ran to the spot, calling her name, but found only a large stone strangely resembling a person. In despair, he stood motionless before the rock as it appeared to change into the form of the merciful Buddha. Soon Asadal began to carve this stone into an image of Buddha which he dedicated to the spirit of his departed wife.

The pond still bears the name of Shadow Pond and a small hermitage with the Buddha image is still there. In sad remembrance of this event the village people began to call the Tabot'ap Pagoda, the Shadow Pagoda. and the Sŏkkat'ap Pagoda, the No Shadow Pagoda.

Sŏkkuram Grotto Shrine

Sŏkkuram is located about 8 kilometers up from the Pulguksa Temple on the top of Mt. Tohamsan. One of the most famous of Korea's cave temples, it was built in 751 by the architect Kim Taesŏng. On several occasions, Sŏkkuram underwent repair work during the Koryŏ and Chosŏn periods. The grotto, however, disappeared from the memory of Koreans until it was rediscovered in 1909.

Sŏkkuram is an artificial grotto with a foreroom, a doorway, and a dome-room. In the dome-room is a granite sitting statue of Shakyamuni on a stone lotus seat. The grotto is entered through the foreroom, which is connected with the principal hall by a corridor. Measuring 6.5 meters in depth, the oblong foreroom is decorated with ten standing figures cut into stone slabs in bas-relief. Three Deva Kings stand along the right and left walls, facing each other. Two more Deva Kings decorate the wall facing the principal hall, one standing at the right and the other at the left. On the wall facing the entrance two more Deva Kings, one at the right and the other at the left, guard the sanctuary.

The Four Heavenly Kings are placed on both walls of the corridor, two at the right and two at the left, facing each other. Two octagonal pillars stand at the entrance of the principal hall, almost round, 7 meters in diameter.

A seated Shakyamuni, the huge main Buddha, occupies the center of the dome-shaped hall, displaying a sublime beauty of harmony. The zenith of Korea's Buddhist sculpture, the main Buddha is surrounded, along the wall, by his 15 disciples. Inside a 25.4 centimeter cut in the upper part of the wall are enshrined seated Bodhisattvas. Above the wall niches is the dome ceiling, which is decorated with a vast lotus flower pattern carved in relief.

In order to appreciate the value of Sŏkkuram, it is necessary to comprehend the place the grotto has in Korea's ancient architecture, and to conduct comparative research on cave temples of India, China, and Korea. Most noteworthy is the geometrical proportion and precision of the Shilla artists' construction at Sŏkkuram. One thousand years have passed since its construction, and their mathematical knowledge and architectural skill is still highly impressive.

The position of the main Buddha is also impressive. The statue is so placed that it is slightly off center in the principal hall. When viewed from the foreroom, it looks as if it occupies the center, on account of the fact that darkness shrouds the statue in the background. The Shilla architects knew how to utilize optical illusion.

Ch'ŏmsŏngdae Astronomical Observatory
(National Treasure No. 105)

In ancient times, in every country of the world natural sciences were represented only by astronomy and meteorology. In Korea in the Shilla period science was fostered, as evidenced by this stone observatory, Ch'ŏmsŏngdae, which was built in 647. It is probably the oldest of the observatories still remaining in East Asia.

The 9.4-meter-high, round edifice, supported by a two-part foundation, consists of 27 levels of granite blocks piled one upon another. The diameter gradually lessens until about two thirds of the way up so that the building resembles a milk bottle. Two square frames are placed on the summit. There are two square windows on the right and left, slightly above the midway point.

P'osŏkjŏng Pavilion

Going southward about 4 kilometers one soon reaches the Five Tombs, and a small, thick pine forest can be seen from there. The forest contains what remains of a detached palace, P'osŏkjŏng, or "Stone Abalone-shaped Pavilion," so named because the arbor housed a banquet place equipped

Punhwangsa Pagoda

P'osŏkjŏng

with an abalone-shaped stone channel through which wine cups were floated during royal parties.

Punhwangsa Pagoda (National Treasure No. 30)

This stone-block pagoda is located on the grounds of Punhwangsa Temple. It was built in 634, during the reign of Queen Sŏndŏk. There were originally nine stories, though now only three remain. This large pagoda was construced with slabs of stone which look like bricks, in imitation of the Chinese-style brick pagodas. On four sides of the first story are doors flanked on either side by scowling Deva guardians. On the four corners of the platform are stone-sculptured lions, the traditional guards of Buddhist scripture.

A gold belt excavated from a Shilla royal tomb (right) and the Divine Bell of the Great King Sŏngdŏk (opposite page) that can be seen at the Kyŏngju National Museum.

Kyŏngju National Museum

Many relics of the Shilla era are on display at this museum. The museum was the display center of the Kyŏngju Relics Preservation Society in 1919 when it was first built. With the liberation in 1945 it became the Kyŏngju branch of the National Museum.

In the garden of the museum are stone relics collected in Kyŏngju and its suburbs: stone pagodas, stone images of Buddha, stone lamps, and tortoise statues.

The Ongogak Pavilion, which was the residence of the magistrate of Kyŏngju during the Chosŏn Kingdom, houses relics representing cultures as far back as the Stone Age and as recent as the Chosŏn period.

In 1921 the Kŭmgwan-go House was built especially to house gold crowns, gold earrings, gold bracelets, gold belts, horse trappings, cases containing the ashes of famous Buddhist monks, and flutes made of precious stone, after a large quantity of these objects were unearthed at the Kŭmgwan Tomb.

Housed in a pavilion on the grounds of the museum is the Divine Bell of Great King Sŏngdŏk, or Emille Bell, the largest and most beautifully resonant bell in the country. The bell was cast in 770, the sixth year of the reign of King Hyegong of Shilla. The bell has a height of 3.33 meters and a diameter of 2.27 meters. To cast such a huge bell many Buddhist monks had to make a tour of the country to raise funds. One of the monks who traveled throughout the country house to house knocked at the gate of a destitute farmer. To the visiting monk, the matron of the house said that, being so poor, she had nothing to contribute but an infant daughter. The monk wrote down what the woman offered in his donation book.

Later when the casting of the bell was begun it was decided that a human sacrifice was necessary. In the history of Buddhism there were many human sacrifices in order to make most holy the items of worship. So the infant daughter of the destitute farm woman was brought and thrown into the pot of melted copper. The bell was finally cast and responded to being struck with a mournful tolling which reminded one of a baby crying "emille...emille..." Hence the name of the bell became "Emille" (meaning "Mommy").

Mt. Sǒraksan and the East Coast

Shinhǔngsa

The eastern coastline, stretching some 390 kilometers from Hwajinp'o Beach south of the Demilitarized Zone down to the port and steel city of P'ohang, is a spectacular range of rugged, peaked mountains and steep gorges that are the course-ways of plunging, cascading streams emptying into the East Sea.

Along the coastal road leading north from Kangnǔng, numerous bathing beaches are crowded with vacationers in summer. The popular beaches are Sokch'o, Naksan, Sǒrak, Hajodae, Chumunjin, and Kyǒngp'odae. The entire coastline is dotted with graceful and weathered old pavilions and temples situated in scenic surroundings.

Just before reaching the coast on the Yongdong Expressway, one encounters Yongp'yǒng, or Dragon Valley Ski Resort, which is equipped with chair lifts, artificial snow-making machines and a ski lodge, thus making this area a year-round resort. Three national parks have been designated along the east coast: Mt. Sǒraksan National Park, the nature lover's paradise of 344 square kilometers of forested ruggedness; Mt. Odaesan National Park, 298.5 square kilometers famous for Woljǒngsa Temple with its octagonal nine-story stone pagoda; and Mt. Chuwangsan National Park at the southern extreme.

The principal resort area is Sǒraksan Mountain, which means "Snow-capped Mountain," in a group of ruggedly beautiful mountains called the "Alps of Asia." Overshadowed by the world-famous Diamond Mountains which lie just to the north, Sǒraksan slumbered in relative obscurity until only a few decades ago. Until 1950, Sǒraksan was in the area under control of North Korea but, with the signing of the armistice in 1953, the demarcation line between the North and the South was drawn north of Sǒraksan, but south of the Diamond Mountains. This fateful act eventually propelled Sǒraksan into the fame it should have earned much sooner. Lack of transportation and ignorance were responsible for its obscurity, for its scenery is on a par with that of the Diamond Mountains.

The Kǔmgangsan, or Diamond Mountains, comprise one of the more scenic spots of the world and the pride of Korea. The Diamond Mountains are located just north of Sǒraksan in North Korea. It is estimated that this spectacular aggregation has some 12,000 peaks; the highest one, Piro Pong, is about 1,820 meters high. The circumference of the mountains is about 81 kilometers. There are clusters of countless rocky peaks in fantastic forms, with primeval forest vegetation below. Crystal clear waters flow through numerous ravines and canyons amidst high rocks of grotesque shapes, forming many beautiful waterfalls. In the days before Korea's division, the Diamond Mountains were a most favored sight for tourists. They remain a symbol to the Korean people that happier days will return when their country is reunited.

The highest peak of Sǒraksan is called Taech'ǒngpong or Great Green, which towers 1,700 meters, making it the second highest peak on the mainland of the Republic of Korea, after the, 1,915-meter-high Mt. Chirisan. Heavily wooded throughout, Sǒraksan is a sylvan paradise of

Mt. Chuwangsan

194

Woljŏngsa

Mt. Sŏraksan

Pisŏndae (above), Ulsanam (right), and Piryong (far right) are the destinations of popular hiking courses.

198

cascading streams, ferns, cliffs, fantastic rock formations and exquisitely rugged scenery.

The distance from Seoul to Sŏraksan is approximately 160 kilometers. The lodge is open year-round, and each season offers different scenery. In the fall, the trees are in their autumnal colors, and in spring, especially in early May, the cherry trees are in full bloom. During summer the thick primeval forest of the Greet Green usually offers a cold mountain breeze to cut the heat, and swimming is available in either crystal clear mountain pools or in the nearby ocean. In winter this area becomes like a crystal wonderland by virtue of all the frozen waterfalls and streams.

There are three popular hiking courses offered by the guided tour service. The destinations of these are Kyejo Hermitage, Pisŏndae or the Flying Promontory, and Piryong, or the Flying Dragon Waterfall. The first hiking course to Kyejo Hermitage covers a distance of about 4 kilometers from the Sŏrak Lodge, passing by Shinhŭngsa Temple on a well established path. The hermitage is a small side temple belonging to Shinhŭngsa and is located in about as picturesque a location as one could hope to find. Against the base of a truly fantastic rock, called Ulsanam, the temple extends underneath into a natural cave. An altar in the inner recesses is reached by a candle-lit path. The view from the Kyejo is fabulous. Off to the south is one of the best views obtainable of Taech'ŏngpong, the highest peak, snowcapped until late May. Also near Kyejo is a large rock called Rocking Rock, which like many of its counterparts in other parts of the world, can easily be rocked by even one person, but cannot be rolled by a force of 100.

The second suggested hike, to Pisŏndae, or the Flying Promontory, is the easiest of the three. Pisŏndae is only about 3.2 kilometers from the lodge, more than half of the distance is on level ground, and the entire course offers no steep sections. Pisŏndae is a towering rock that rises almost perpendicularly at the entrance to a most beautiful gorge. Heavily wooded, with pines and other trees growing out of the most improbable places, the narrow gorge is set off by a dashing stream that tumbles and spills over tremendous boulders, sometimes in rapids, and sometimes taking breathers in limpid, mirror clear pools.

The third of the three basic hikes, to Flying Dragon Waterfall, is the hardest of the three but was recently made much easier by the completion of a suspension bridge over the most difficult spot. Again about 3.2 kilometers from the lodge, the path winds its way up an even narrower gorge than in the case of Pisŏndae. The goal, Flying Dragon Waterfall, is, as its name suggests, a waterfall that resembles a flying dragon. The rock over which the stream spills to form this waterfall is so evenly shaped that it looks more manmade than natural. The pool at the base is extremely deep and ideal for swimming, except that the water is quite chilly until late June.

The ocean side of Sŏraksan is called Outer Sŏrak and the western mountain side, Inner Sŏrak. A hike to the top of the mountain and then down to the ocean beach requires several days. For maximum appreciation, a day should be allowed for each hike. But if pressed for time, the hiker can complete all three courses in one day or a day and a half.

Within five minutes walking distance of the Sŏrak lodge is Shinhŭngsa Temple, built during the Shilla Kingdom in the seventh century. The complex of buildings offers genuine Korean architecture at its best. Surrounded by steep mountains on all sides, the temple also offers a clear mountain stream which flows over tremendous boulders just in front of the main building.

Mt. Hallasan

Chejudo Islands

The islands of Chejudo consist of the southernmost and largest island of Korea, neighboring islets, and the Chuja Islands. The distance between the main island and Mokp'o on the mainland is approximately 140 kilometers, and that between Chejudo and Pusan, the port city on the southeastern tip of the peninsula, is 259 kilometers.

Its area is 1,820 square kilometers, and it is shaped in the form of an oval 73 kilometers from east to west and 41 kilometers from north to south. With Mt. Hallasan at 1,950 meters standing slightly west and south of the true midpoint of the island, Chejudo's circumference is about 253 kilometers, its annual mean temperature is 15 degrees centigrade, and its average rainfall is 1,440 millimeters.

Not only does Chejudo have in Mt. Hallasan the highest mountain in South Korea, but it also may claim uniqueness in the 360 parasite volcanoes scattered over the island. These parasite volcanoes give the landscape an almost lunar appearance, especially in the early morning or late evening. The inclination of the southern foot, however, is more abrupt than that of the northern area, therefore, the southern coastline has many precipices. The eastern and western ends have wider plains than the southern and northern ends, and the southwestern coastal area boasts the broadest plain on the island. It is believed that volcanic eruptions started toward the end of the third geological era, with coarse-grained rocks erupting in the beginning, and continued through the 41st era until finally, explosive eruptions occurred followed by a flow of great basalt lava streams. Repeated eruptions formed the volcanic topography.

Before the Christian era, Chejudo was an independent state called Chuho, and during the Three Kingdoms period it was called T'amna. T'amna then traded with the Paekche Kingdom, but later became part of the Unified Shilla Kingdom.

The Chejudo Islands are also known by the name Samdado, which means "Islands Abundant in Three Things," namely rocks, wind, and women. Perhaps the most exotic and interesting sight on Chejudo are the diving women. Until the late 1960s there were approximately 30,000 women divers who supported their families with the riches of the island's coastal sea where they explored. The number of these stalwart amazons, however, has been gradually decreasing.

The island is famous for its many natural resources such as fish, shellfish and seaweed. Also many plants of the temperate and tropical zones grow in Chejudo. Among them, the sub-tropical tangerine, banana, pineapple, and papaya plants are cultivated.

Chejudo is ideal for the cultivation of mushrooms. Lacking extreme temperatures and blessed with many naturally air-conditioned caves, it is conceivable that Chejudo can become one of the world's principal mushroom raising areas.

Last, but not least, Chejudo has the right combination of factors to become an important tourist center in Eastern Asia.

Hallasan Mountain

Mt. Hallasan, rising hundreds of meters above sea level, is the second highest mountain in Korea next to Mt. Paektusan, and is regarded as one of the three most sacred mountains in the country. The other two are Mt. Kŭmgangsan and Mt. Chirisan.

A stone harubang.

On the top of Mt. Hallasan is a crater which has become a large natural lake called Paengnokdam, meaning "White Deer Lake," and is so named because of an old legend which says a divine spirit once spent time here with a white deer. The lake and basin are formed by the mouth of the extinct volcano that is Mt. Hallasan.

Snow that covers the lake area in winter and remains until May creates one of "the ten famous landscapes" often referred to as a "scene of late snow on the Deer Lake."

Going down the mountain ridge about 4 kilometers southwest from the peak, one can find an infinite variety of rare and odd rocks of various shapes and sizes lining up as if supporting the sky. The rocks, called "Five Hundred Generals" or "Five Hundred Arhats" because they resemble many generals lined up together, create a spectacular scene in the midst of the surrounding dense vegetation and trees.

Samsŏnghyŏl or the Shrine of the Three Progenitors

Samsŏnghyŏl is the most sacred spot on Chejudo. According to legend, about 2,000 years ago three semi-divine men came out of the ground here and became the progenitors of the Chejudo people. A group of classic Korean-style buildings exists here which are to this day used for periodic ancestral ceremonies by the clans of Ko, Yang, and Pu, the purported present-day descendants of the three semi-divine forefathers.

Harubang or Stone Images

The oldest *harubang* is called Usŏngmong and is one of the formative artistic works which shows a true aspect of Chejudo. The *harubang* are crudely carved in the shape of human figures with large eyeballs and hands resting on the stomach. The time of their construction is not known, but, according to existing available records, it is conjectured that they were constructed about 210 years ago. The best examples of *harubang* are to be found in Cheju City at the entrance to Samsŏnghyŏl, near the entrance to the museum. A *harubang* image customarily was erected at the entrance to a village and deemed the guardian deity of the village. Also, it was believed to prevent disaster.

Waterfalls

Chŏngbang Waterfall is 28 meters high and is distinctive in that it falls almost directly into the sea. A staircase permits the sightseer to descend to its base. The coast in this area is rugged and most majestic.

Ch'ŏnjiyŏn is another waterfall just west of the town of Sŏgwip'o. At the head of a narrow gorge, this waterfall is surrounded by luxuriant vegetation, including many Oriental cherry trees. The pool below is surrounded by ferns and evergreens and is the habitat of the conger eel, its worldwide northernmost penetration. The winding cliffs here are quite majestic with their curious rocks.

Ch'ŏnjeyŏn Waterfall also is located near the town of Sŏgwip'o. There are three waterfalls, the upper one rarely actually having water. The pool at the base, however, is fed by underground streams and is a curious deep blue color. The lower two waterfalls are lacy and always have water. By its scale, Ch'ŏnjeyŏn deserves to be called "The Niagara of Korea."

Paengnokdam

Ilchulbong

Women divers

Mt. Chirisan National Park

Songgwangsa

A three-story stone pagoda in Hwaŏmsa

The largest national park in Korea, Mt. Chirisan National Park covers an area of 438.9 square kilometers, and the mountains themselves have four majestic peaks: Ch'ŏnwangbong (1,915m), Panyabong (1,751m), Sesŏkpong (1,437m), and Nogodan (1,506m above sea level).

Besides scenic beauty, this area is famous for Buddhist temples scattered around the mountain's base; some of the most famous are Hwaŏmsa, Shilsangsa, Ssanggyesa, Sŏnamsa, Ch'ŏnŭnsa, and Songgwangsa.

Hwaŏmsa, originally built in 528, was renovated by Priest Ŭisang in 670 as his headquarters of Avatamsaka Buddhism in Korea, from which the name of this temple, Hwaŏmsa, derived. The temple underwent repairs and renovations several times until it was burnt down during the Japanese invasion of Korea in 1592, and it was not rebuilt until 1636.

Kakhwangjŏn, the main hall which is 12.7 meters across the front and 9 meters on the sides, is one of the largest temple buildings in Korea. It was built between 1696 and 1703, and subsequently became the center of both Zen and Doctrinaire Buddhism when the two sects were merged into one. The stone lantern in front of the main hall is the tallest one in Korea, measuring 6.4 meters in height and 2.8 meters in diameter. It has been designated National Treasure No. 12. Two five-story pagodas, one called East Pagoda and the other West Pagoda, stand in front of the main hall facing each other. A three-story stone pagoda with four lions, also located here, is said to have been built by Zen Master Yŏnggi as a memorial to his deceased mother. The four lions, one at each of the four corners, support the body of the pagoda. There are, in Korea, six stone lanterns and pagodas supported by lions, but none of them can quite compare with the pagoda here.

Ch'ŏnŭnsa, which lies west of Mt. Chirisan, was originally built in 811, but the present buildings are of an 18th century reconstruction. The former name of the temple was Kamnosa, meaning "sweet dew," because there was a fountain of medicinal waters in its precincts. The present name,

Hwaŏmsa

Sŏnamsa

Ssanggyesa

Songgwangsa (below)

Mt. Chirisan

A bridge at Sŏnamsa

Ch'ŏnŭnsa, meaning "hidden fountain," was given after the well dried up. Ssanggyesa Temple is located on the southern slope of Mt. Chirisan, and was built in 723. The temple is renowned for the stone monument for Priest Chin-gam, which was erected in 887; the inscription on the monument is said to have been written by Ch'oe Ch'i-won, a great scholar of the Shilla period.

Songgwangsa is the largest Buddhist monastery in Korea, reputed to have housed 3,000 monks at one time, but many of its buildings were burnt down in 1948 when a community-inspired military revolt occurred in the area. Among the 50-odd buildings, Kiksajŏn Hall, which was built in the early days of the Chosŏn Kingdom, is designated National Treasure No. 56.

Sŏnamsa lies near Songgwangsa which was built by Priest Tosŏn during the latter days of the Shilla period. The temple still has some ten buildings, of which Wont'ongjŏn is unique.

Yŏngoksa Temple was originally built in 544, but most of its buildings were burnt down during the Korean War and it has been rebuilt since then. Three stone stupas of the Koryŏ period still attract many believers and sightseers to this temple. Two of them, the East Stupa and the North Stupa, have been designated National Treasures Nos. 53 and 54.

Shilsangsa Temple is delightful, snugly set at the foot of Mt. Chirisan and right on the banks of the upper reaches of the Sŏmjin-gang River. The temple was originally built in 828, but the present buildings were rebuilt in 1681 and 1715. There are two Shilla pagodas and many stone monuments and stone stupas; among them the three-story pagoda at Paekchang-am Hermitage, which is believed to have been built in the ninth century, has been designated National Treasure No. 10.

Mt. Chirisan covers a large territory and forms the boundary of three provinces in South Korea. The mountains teem with vegetable and animal life, including musk oxen, 22 other species of mammals, 163 species of birds and many medicinal herbs, plus tea. Most of the temples described above have tea farms, small and large.

Shilsangsa

Stupa at Yŏngoksa

Monument remains at Yŏngoksa

Sŏnamsa (below)

Mt. Kyeryongsan National Park

This is the nearest national park to Seoul, about a two-hour train ride from the capital to Taejŏn, and about half an hour's drive from there to Tonghaksa Temple at the foot of the mountain. This area, covering some 61 square kilometers, was designated a national park in 1968. The mountain is so named because it resembles a wriggling dragon with the crest of a cock. The highest peak, Sangbong, is 827 meters above sea level. This area is known as one of the five most scenic mountains in Korea.

Mt. Kyeryongsan has long been known as the mecca of new religions, with more than 40 sects, large and small, of mixed doctrines, scattered around a village called Shindoan. T'aejo, the founder-king of the Chosŏn Kingdom, once comtemplated building his new capital on this mountain, and work was started in 1393 which was, however, later suspended. Forty-two foundation stones that were laid down at that time can still be seen there.

Tonghaksa Temple, which is said to have been built by Priest Toson during the Unified Shilla period, is a gateway to this mysterious mountain. However, what has made this temple renowned from ancient times is the fact that it has been used by famous men in offering sacrificial rites to loyal subjects. Kil Chae, the famous poet and scholar of the 14th century, offered prayer here for Chŏng Mong-chu, the last loyal subject of the fallen Koryŏ Kingdom, who was killed by assassins of the new kingdom. Kim Shi-sŭp, a famous novelist of the 16th century, also offered prayers at the temple to the so-called Six Martyrs. Seasonal offerings are still made in spring and autumn.

About 1.5 kilometers above the valley is the Ŭnsŏn Falls, on the way to another famous temple, Kapsa, about 6 kilometers toward Kongju. Kapsa Temple was built in 556, but the present wooden buildings are recent reconstructions except for the stone and iron flagpole, which was erected in 697, and the stone stupa of the Koryŏ period.

Down the slope toward the west lies Puyŏ, the last capital of Paekche from 538 to 660, when the kingdom was destroyed by Shilla. However, unlike Kyŏngju, Puyŏ has few relics of the time. The Puyŏ branch of the National Museum was built recently to house and to display historical remains collected and excavated from this area. Kongju made big news in July 1971 when the tomb of Paekche King Muryŏng-wang was accidentally discovered and excavated. The tomb yielded many relics, including two gold crowns, and enough gold earrings, gold caskets, armlets, and hair pins to fill a separate museum. The most important items, however, were the tomb stones which precisely stated the name, the burial date of the deceased, and that Muryŏng-wang ruled the kingdom from 501-523. The tomb is open to the public, and most of the burial objects discovered in the tomb chambers are displayed in the museum.

Tonghaksa (top) and Kapsa (right) are two of the major temples located in the Kyeryongsan vicinity.

210

Hallyŏ Waterway National Park

The Hallyŏ Sudo, literally meaning "waterway" linking Hansando Island and Yŏsu, is a unique inland sea area famed for its natural beauty, dotted with nearly 400 islands, small and large, on the calm and glassy waters off the southern coast. These islands sprinkled across the sea form a 200-kilometer-long archipelago. This area is known as one of the Eight Wonders of Scenic Beauty. This maritime national park is dotted with picturesque islets, quaint fishing boats, and traditional seaside villages which support an intensive oyster-raising industry. Visitors often hear local people boast of historical artifacts, especially those related to Admiral Yi Sun-shin. One can visit historical sites related to Admiral Yi scattered around this area by taking a boat plying between Pusan and Yŏsu.

Pusan has a huge harbor, one of the finest and largest natural harbors in the Far East. The seaport city, sprawling over the hills and valleys surrounding the site, has a population of some four million. Some 450 kilometers from Seoul, Pusan is the main gateway to Korea from Japan and the United States by sea, and the southern terminal of Korea's main railway system. The harbor is excellently protected by many islands, large and small. The port presents a forest of colorful masts, with foreign ships intermingled with domestic liners and fishing boats.

Mount Yongdusan (literally meaning Dragon Head Mountain), rising in the heart of the city, is a park commanding a view of the picturesque southern area, and even Tsushima Island looms on the horizon in fine weather. Songdo or Pine Tree Island, 2 kilometers south of the downtown city, is a peninsula beach noted for sea-bathing in the summer season.

On the eastern outskirts of Pusan, in the direction of Haeundae Spa, is the United Nations Cemetery. There lie many of the valiant soldiers and sailors dispatched from the 16 United Nations member nations who gave their lives during the Korean War (1950-53) in defense of freedom and democracy. Haeundae Beach, some 22 kilometers east of downtown Pusan, is a fine summer seaside resort providing bathing facilities and hot springs.

The southern coastline, linking Pusan and Yŏsu, is inlaid with emerald islets which shine in the sun like a long string of sparkling gems. Especially admirable is the view of the long channel stretching between Hansando Island and Yŏsu, and foreign tourists often make sightseeing voyages through this archipelago area, which is called Tadohae, the "Sea with Many Islands."

A voyage of one and a half hours from Pusan will take one to Chinhae, an important, naturally favored naval port. The major area of the city is occupied by naval forces in an encampment of the Korean naval educational center. Chinhae is noted for the Naval Academy and the presidential summer villa. Foreign dignitaries and domestic celebrities often visit this place to hold various meetings, as well as to enjoy the serene beauty of the landscape.

Cherry trees, numbering nearly 10,000, symbolically herald the spring season by their initial blooming. The road from Pukwon Rotary leading up to the front gate of the Naval Academy forms a tunnel of flowers during the spring season.

Since the unveiling ceremony of Admiral Yi's bronze statue on April 13, 1951, the naval port has been open to the public for annual week-long festivities. Chewang Park in the central part of the city is covered

Pusan Harbor

The United Nations Cemetery (below)   Chinhae (below)

A statue of Admiral Yi Sun-shin

with dense forests, and the steps, numbering 365, which lead from the foot of the mountain up to the peak, have the interesting nickname of "One Year Steps." Legend has it that any woman who wishes to have a baby may realize her wish only when she follows all 365 steps to the top of the mountain.

Ch'ungmu is noted for its abundant records and relics concerned with Admiral Yi's naval victory during the Hideyoshi Invasion. History tells us that Admiral Yi fought the enemy in the narrow strait between Hansando and Kŏjedo islands, destroying 73 Japanese vessels before returning to his naval base in T'ong-yŏng. According to the records the enemy lost 220 ships, and 590 sailors were drowned in a series of engagements on the sea.

The Sebyŏnggwan Pavilion has been designated by the government as National Treasure No. 447. History tells us that the navy men washed their blood-stained swords here upon returning from a fight against the Japanese invaders.

The bronze statue of Admiral Yi Sun-shin, in full armor with his sword, stands majestically on Namgang Mountain (literally meaning "Viewing Southward") overlooking the scenes of his great victories at sea. Anyone who visits Ch'ungmu will visit Chungyŏlsa, a memorial shrine dedicated to the great admiral.

Connecting Ch'ungmu City to an adjacent island is a 461-meter-long subsea tunnel. This is the only one of its kind in Korea. As it is one of the major stops for shuttle steamships operating between Pusan and Yŏsu, vacationers are frequently here both in the summer and winter seasons.

Hansando Island lies between Ch'ungmu and Kŏjedo Island, Korea's second largest island, of 392 square kilometers. King Sŏnjo, the 26th king of the Chosŏn Kingdom, ordered the building of Chesŏngdang Pavilion and established headquarters for navy men under Admiral Yi. This small

The Hallyŏ Waterway

216

island has been designated Historical Site No. 113 by the government.

On Namhaedo Island, Kŭmsan Mountain and its vicinity provide the scenic beauties of rocky mountains with many cliffs and immense dark forests on precipitous hills. Kŭmsan's height is 681 meters, rising high above the southern tip of the island. Legend has it that the great Buddhist priest Wonhyo built Pogwangsa Temple here and this mountain once had the name of Pogwang Mountain. Later the first king of the Chosŏn Kingdom, T'aejo (Yi Sŏng-gye), gave it another name, Kŭmsan, chiefly because he himself visited there to perform a 100-day-long prayer service, through which he at last rose to become the kingdom's founding king.

From the peak of the mountain one can look down on the overall scene of the town of Namhae, and can also view the wide sea dotted with small islands leading to Yŏsu. Around the hillside of this mountain, visitors will find a stone monument erected to honor 11 U.S. Air Force crewmen who died in a B-29 airplane which crashed on the mountain during the Korean War.

The Yŏsu district boasts an abundance of marine products, such as laver, sea shells, seaweed and anchovies. The local people have high hopes of prosperity, since the government has designated the district as an industrial complex area. Even though the island seaway around the Yŏsu district is yet to be developed, the tourism potential is very high.

In the center of Yŏsu City, a pavilion named Chinnamgwan deserves close observation for those who have an interest in Korea's traditional architecture. The columns used for this pavilion are said to have been brought from Mt. Chirisan. It was originally built for receiving officials and holding ceremonies and was later used for a military training center.

Just 1 kilometer beyond the seashore is Odongdo Island, which is surrounded by groves of camellia and bamboo. A lengthy dike linking Yŏsu to the island stretches 720 meters. At dusk the sunset view from the island is superb.

Haegŭmgang

Hongdo Island

*The P'alsangjŏn and image
of Buddha for which
Pŏpchusa is most famous.*

Mt. Songnisan National Park

Mt. Songnisan is about a three-hour's drive from Seoul. Mt. Songnisan is 1,057 meters high and is one of the most famous scenic places in the nation. Also this area has many historical relics and natural monuments. The mountains around the area are exquisite in their fall array of brilliant colors, or in their summer garb of pastel wild flowers.

There are nine peaks, called Kubong, with thick forests of old pine trees and strange-looking rocks scattered about. With the Ch'ŏnhwangbong or Imperial Peak as their chief summit, several of the mountains line up in a bow-like shape to the north. The Yŏngch'ŏn River, a branch of the Kŭmgang River, originates here. The famous Pŏpchusa Temple, embowered in pine woods, was once the largest temple in Korea and is known to have hosted some 30,000 priests at one gathering. The foliage in the forests is so thick that the place is dark even during the daytime.

Pŏpchusa Temple was built by a priest named Ŭisang Chosa during the reign of King Chinhŭng of Shilla, about 1,400 years ago. The temple was repaired eight times during the Koryŏ and Chosŏn Kingdoms, and the number of Buddhist monks at the temple is said to have once reached 3,000. Only a few dozen monks guard the temple at the present time.

Objects on the temple grounds designated as national treasures include a wooden five-story building called P'alsangjŏn, a stone lamp with two lions, Sŏngyŏnji, a stone lamp with carved devas, or watchmen, and a Buddha statue. A Devas gate and a stone statue of Buddha are widely known relics. There are also many hermitages, or small temples, in every valley of these mountains. Especially significant is the image of Buddha that was unveiled there on June 14, 1964, which is the largest in Asia. The image is 29 meters high. There are four stone lamp stands on the grounds of Pŏpchusa, the oldest of their kind in the nation. This temple became famous as successive kings visited it frequently.

There are three natural monuments: a white pine tree at Oam-ri, a manggae tree at Sannae-ri, and a pine tree with the rank of cabinet minister standing at Sangbang-ri, all near the P'opchusa Temple. The most famous of the three natural monuments is the pine tree with cabinet minister rank. There is an anecdote about how the tree was awarded such high standing. When King Sejo of the Chosŏn Kingdom was traveling to Pŏpchusa Temple, he granted the tree the rank of cabinet minister as a token of his thanks for the shelter it provided when he and his procession were caught in a big thunderstorm.

Relics of Pŏpchusa Temple

The Twin Lion Stone Lamp (National Treasure No. 5) is 3.3 meters high. Twin lions, standing erect on their hind legs support a middle rack with their forelegs. Lotus flowers are engraved on a stone under their feet, and petals of lotus flowers are also engraved around the middle rack. There is an octagonal compartment in which to place a torch, and a precious stone is set in the lid. This is a well-balanced, beautiful lamp, a masterpiece superior to all other stone lamps made during the Shilla Kingdom.

Devas Stone Lamp   *Sŏngnyŏnji*

Devas Stone Lamp (National Treasure No. 15)

This lamp stands 4 meters high and is made of granite. Four Devas are magnificently sculptured on it, and various floral designs are engraved on its middle stone, with petals of lotus flowers engraved on its lower stone. This lamp also displays the Shilla techniques of sculpture.

P'alsangjŏn (National Treausre No. 55)

This five-story main building, the only one of its kind in the nation, has many unique architectural characteristics. The wooden pillar at its center rises up to the roof and the iron pole on its roof plays the role of a lightening rod. Inside the building, a picture series hanging on the four walls describes the life of Buddha.

Sŏngnyŏnji (National Treasure No. 64)

This sculpture completed in 720 is 1,095 meters high and 66.5 meters in circumference. It symbolizes the Lotus Pond of Paradise. All lotus flowers on this sculpture are carved out of granite. It is supported by lotus-shaped sculptures, and there are curlicued foundation stones. It is thought that the lotus flower, one that remains always clean and uncontaminated, urges the people to return to their original august virtues.

Haeinsa Temple in Mt. Kayasan

Haeinsa Temple is located deep in Mt. Kayasan, about 64 kilometers northwest of Taegu. Crystal clear rivulets rumble down from Mt. Kayasan through strange rock formations and age-old pines, in places forming spectacular waterfalls. On the way to the temple is a pavilion built on the site where the great Shilla scholar Ch'oe Ch'i-won lived with his family after the fall of Shilla.

The temple is recorded to have been built in 802 by priests Sunŭng and Ijŏng during the Shilla Kingdom. The original main hall was a large three-story wooden structure, but the present one was built toward the end of the Chosŏn Kingdom.

The stone steps behind the main hall lead to two wooden buildings, store-houses for the world famous *Tripitaka Koreana* which has been designated a national treasure. The storehouses, known as Changgyŏngpan-go, were built in 1488 to store the 81,258 wooden blocks carved on both sides with the 80,000 Buddhist sutras and canons which were engraved for printing between 1237 and 1252.

This *Tripitaka Koreana* is not only the oldest in the world but also a more complete and standard Buddhist bible than any found in China, Japan or any other Buddhist country in the East. It was preserved on Kanghwado Island until it was moved to this temple in the late 15th century.

Eleven small subordinate hermitages surround Haeinsa Temple. In front of the main hall stands Wondang-am Hermitage where the founding priests of the main temple resided, and which commands a superb view of the main hall and the storehouses of the *Tripitaka Koreana*. Around this area roof tiles believed to have been made during the Shilla period are still found.

Another path leads from behind the main hall of Haeinsa Temple to Paengnyŏnam Hermitage, about 1 kilometer southeast of the temple. It is a small temple where many Zen meditators sit year-round. Down the slope from this hermitage are two other hermitages Kugilam and Yaksaam. Both are residences and study halls for nuns; the former for the Zen education of nuns, and the latter for girls aspiring to become nuns. High Priest Yujŏng (Samyŏngdang), who commanded a contingent of militant monks during Hideyoshi's invasion of Korea, died in Kugilam Hermitage in 1610. His memorial stone statue, which the local Japanese police destroyed in the 1940s, was reassembled and erected alongside a stream beside the hermitage.

The entrance to the library where the Tripitaka Koreana *wood blocks are kept.*

INDEX

223